35⁰⁰

?7 2003

rge

HARLEM ON THE VERGE

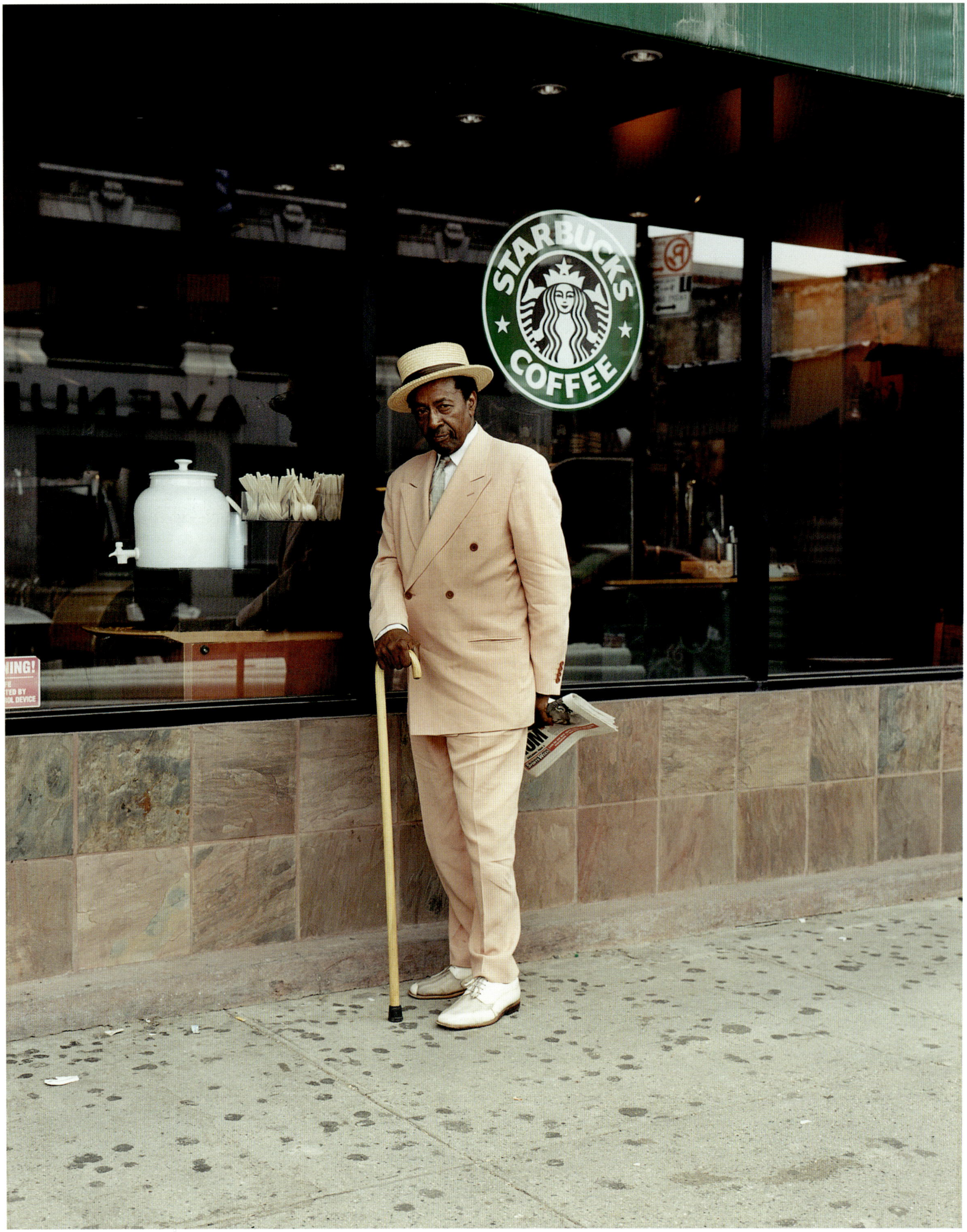
STARBUCKS
COFFEE

ALICE ATTIE

HARLEM ON THE VERGE

INTRODUCTION BY ROBIN D. G. KELLEY

THE QUANTUCK LANE PRESS NEW YORK

First edition

Printed and bound in Italy

Design by Katy Homans
Manufacturing by Mondadori Printing, Verona

ISBN 0-9714548-7-6

Library of Congress Cataloging-in-Publication Data

Attie, Alice.
Harlem : on the verge / Alice Attie ; introduction by Robin D. G. Kelley.— 1st ed.
p. cm.
ISBN 0-9714548-7-6
1. Harlem (New York, N.Y.)—Pictorial works. 2. New York (N.Y.)—Pictorial works. 3. African American neighborhoods—New York (State)—New York—Pictorial works. I. Title.
F128.68.H3A87 2003
974.7'1—dc21
2003009850

THE QUANTUCK LANE PRESS
Distributed by
W. W. Norton & Company, Inc.
500 Fifth Avenue, New York, NY 10110
www.wwnorton.com

W. W. Norton & Company Ltd.,
Castle House, 75/76 Wells Street, London W1T 3QT

1 2 3 4 5 6 7 8 9 0

CONTENTS

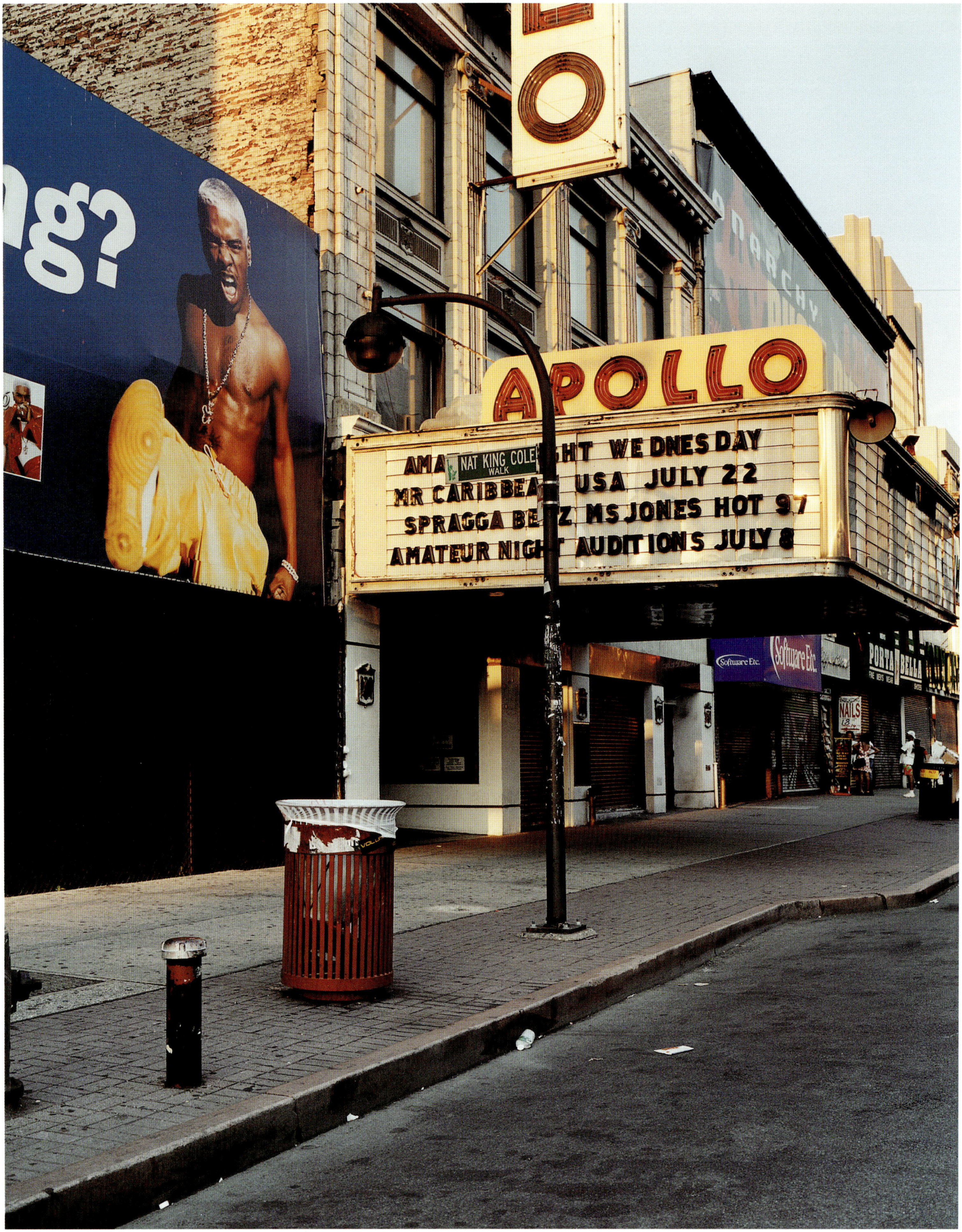
ng?
APOLLO
AMA GHT WEDNESDAY
NAT KING COLE
WALK
MR CARIBBEA USA JULY 22
SPRAGGA BE Z MS JONES HOT 97
AMATEUR NIGHT AUDITIONS JULY 8
Software Etc.
Software Etc.
NAILS
PORTA BELLA

for my parents, Muriel and Joseph

and

my children, Justine and Gideon

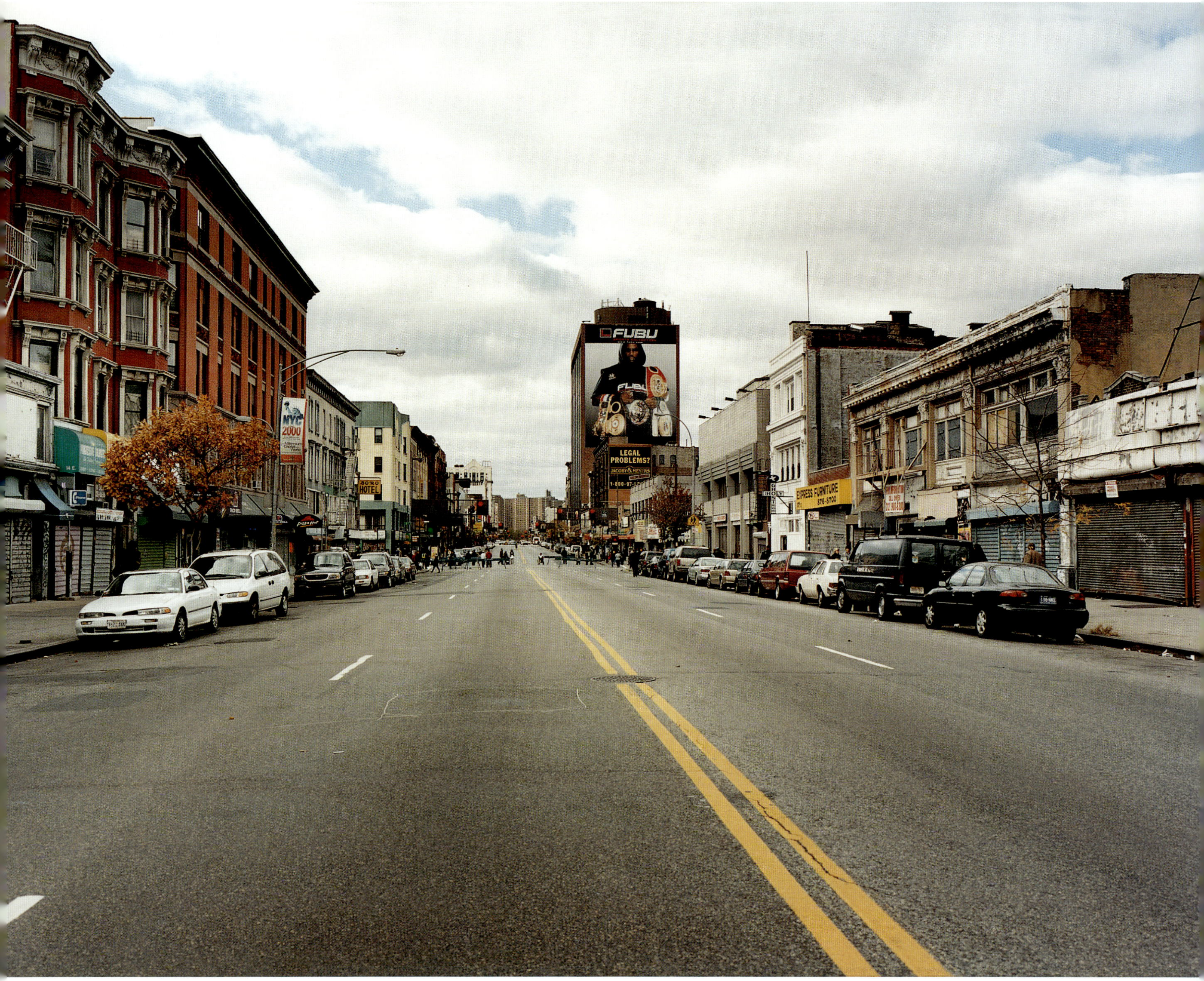
FUBU
LEGAL PROBLEMS?
JACOBY & MEYERS
NYC 2000
HOTEL
EXPRESS FURNITURE
876-8700

DISAPPEARING ACTS: CAPTURING HARLEM IN TRANSITION

ROBIN D. G. KELLEY

"It's like we don't exist any more and those of us who do exist are constantly looking for money to survive."
—BARBARA ANN TEER, founder of the National Black Theater in Harlem[1]

I like to think of Alice Attie's camera as a kind of x-ray machine, penetrating beneath the surface of the current Harlem-mania in order to expose the past and future in the signs and crumbling edifices that have yet to succumb to global capital's demolition ball. These signs, and the buildings to which they are attached, are not merely lost artifacts but declarations of war, holdouts that remind the observant passer-by what black Harlem was and could have been. If these buildings are indeed "records," Attie's camera makes them legible: locating the ideas, visions, and hopes of the people in brownstone, brick, and mortar, in the official and unofficial graffiti which dot the urban landscape. Her x-ray photos reveal the signs of tension between capital's designs for this section of upper Manhattan and the designs of the residents. *Love Nest*, *Pretty City Cocktails*, *Ralph and Son Barber Shop*, *Virgo Beauty Salon* were among the holdouts which found their way into Attie's viewfiender, intimate spaces designated for community building, for romantic encounters, bitch sessions, crying the blues. Places like these are where black working-class life is lived.

Attie has a spectacular eye for reading the irony on the wall. In one photograph, a young woman passes a locked storefront and a wall of posters displaying advertisements for Steve Madden shoes, DMX's latest album, *the Source* magazine, a new release by Wendy, and a post-9/11 poster identifying the police and fire departments as "Our Heroes." Given the history of violence and brutality meted out to black Harlem residents by New York's finest, one suspects that only a severe case of collective amnesia could convince the neighborhood to take this sign seriously. To the right of these posters, painted on the metal storefront gate, is a warning against such amnesia. The painting, by aerosol artist Franco the Great, is of a teary-eyed Dr. King who is telling us to *"Remember . . . I Had a Dream. . . . It's for YOU to Finish it!"*

She presents us with many other spectacles of irony. Consider the abandoned, dilapidated motel invisible to speeding motorists on the West Side Highway. It functions mainly to prop up a sign promoting Continental Airlines and the idea that "There is No Place Like Home." (Is that really "Derrida" scrawled on the motel wall? A post-structuralist gesture, or a marking of territory by the new Harlemites, or both? There goes the neighborhood!) The fact that "Beauty Barber" is underscored by the tag "2 small" creates, in my mind at least, one of those unintentional juxtapositions that speaks to the bulldozer mentality of global capital. The old beauty shop is, indeed, "too small" in the face of a corporate culture that destroys local businesses and institutions in place of a simulacra of the idealized locale.

These signs reveal, too, that history is contested, and that for black residents the glory that was Harlem was more than just a colorful backdrop to enhance neighborhood charm. On the contrary, the past has always been about charting a new future. After all, this place has been labeled "the Negro Mecca", once the most important black city in the entire world. It offered hope for a new beginning in an age of scientific racism barely two generations removed from slavery. It promised the flowering of a black intelligentsia and culture, a symbol of what sophisticated, urbane black people can become if they held power and were left alone. Indeed, it is precisely this sense of hope, possibility, dreams unrealized, that explains why every generation since the early twentieth century laments the loss of "the old Harlem." James Baldwin's memories of the Harlem riots, Claude Brown's lamentations over the introduction of heroin and the rise of crime, Ralph Ellison's reminiscences of the old Minton's Playhouse, John Henrik Clarke's 1964 anthology *Harlem in Transition* all recall the golden age as a thing of the past.[2]

But what was really lost and what will the new Harlem bring? To answer these questions, we need to dig even deeper beneath the surface of these already penetrating photos and figure out how Harlem evolved from mecca to market.

"ARE THE NEGROES GOING TO BE ABLE TO HOLD HARLEM?"

The great poet/critic James Weldon Johnson asked this question way back in 1925. Johnson knew that the great black Renaissance would not last forever. He was less than sanguine about the black community's future in Harlem, predicting that an inevitable rise in land values will force black residents further north and perhaps out of Manhattan altogether. At the same time, he believed that the success of Harlem's black middle class was irreversible, and if white folks had any plans to re-take the old North Manhattan suburb it would cost them. "[T]he Negro's situation in Harlem," Johnson surmised, "is without precedent in all his history in New York; never before has he been so securely anchored, never before has he owned the land, never before has he had so well-established community life. It is probable that land throughout the heart of Harlem will some day so increase in value that Negroes may not be able to hold it—although it is quite as probable that there will be some Negroes able to take full advantage of the increased values—and will be forced to make a move. But the next move, when it comes, will be unlike the others. It will not be a move made solely at the behest of someone else; it will be more in the nature of a bargain."[3]

Today, at the turn of a new century, Harlem is being overrun with bargain hunters in search of dilapidated brownstones and row houses, the kind of housing stock that allows one to make a dream home in an overcrowded real estate market or turn a quick profit through re-sale. *The New York Times*, *New York* magazine, the *Village Voice*, and virtually any publication with its eye on New York have pronounced Harlem the hottest real estate market in the city, thus adding to the skyrocketing value of property. Meanwhile, long-time black and Latino residents, from young mothers to the elderly to local entrepreneurs, are finding themselves on the losing end of the "bargain." Priced out, displaced, gentrified, the old Harlemites who have for so long lurked in the white imagination as a source of fear and fascination have begun to disappear. And yet, as this new army of developers, speculators, and investors march through Harlem behind the wrecking ball of global capital, they are banking on the neighborhood's rich history as the center of black culture and art.

Anyone familiar with the transformation of Harlem today would find James Weldon Johnson's prediction prescient, to say the least. In 1925, Harlem had been deemed by some the capital of the black world, where black artists, intellectuals, and entrepreneurs thrived, black police officers walked the beat, and black dreams need not be deferred. Of course, just three decades before the "Harlem Renaissance," no one would have predicted that the choice block of land from 110th to 145th streets would become a predominantly black community, let alone the epicenter of the African Diaspora. By the turn of the twentieth century, Harlem had become the jewel in Manhattan's crown. Rising land values, boosted by the extension of the IRT, attracted Manhattan's bourgeoisie along with a bevy of real estate speculators who erected beautiful brownstones, luxury apartment buildings, and a few small mansions. Oscar Hammerstein I, who made quite a fortune buying and selling Harlem property, built the Harlem Opera House with the assumption that the elite was there to stay. William Waldorf Astor must have believed the same, for he sank a cool $500,000 into a luxury apartment building on 7th Avenue.[4]

When the editor of the *Harlem Monthly Review* observed that Harlem would become "the centre of fashion, wealth, culture, and intelligence," he was not thinking about Langston Hughes, W. E. B. DuBois, Madame C. J. Walker, or other black "Renaissance" figures. Indeed, had you walked into most Harlem realty companies circa 1900 and you're likely to find a sign on the wall that reads: "The agents promise their tenants that these houses will be rented only to WHITE people." Or you might see the following attached to vacancy notices: "Keine Juden, und keine Hunde" [No Jews, No Dogs]. Yet, when the bottom fell out of the market, these same realtors sold to anyone willing to buy . . . and the rest, as they say, is history.[5]

At the dawn of the twenty-first century, this historic black working-class community threatens to become Manhattan's newest "yuppie mecca." Developers and real estate agents who stand to gain a pretty penny are calling it the "second Harlem renaissance." Between 1990 and 1997, people moving into Harlem making over $75,000 increased by eighty percent, while families earning less than $10,000 decreased by twenty-six percent. But poverty still rules in Harlem. In 1999, the median family income was a paltry $18,000, and lots of folks were still living in overcrowded housing projects and struggling to find work. The unemployment rate hovered around 18 percent—four times the national average. In 2002, despite the influx of more middle and high income earners, the median family income rose slightly to $26,000 per year. Brownstones sell for $800,000 or more, and gutted brownstones begin at $300,000. Rents have tripled. Employed, stable residents who were renting apartments for $500 per month were suddenly being told that they would have to put out $1300 to $1500. In the new Harlem market, one would have to earn approximately $90,000 per year to afford what is considered "moderate-income" housing.[6]

Now there is nothing inherently wrong with rising property values. On the contrary, rising property values are generally good for community development, especially if a substantial portion of the community own their own property.[7] But for so long Harlem was a land of absentee landlords and tenants who lived near or below the poverty line. Without a strategy to create low-income housing units, the increase in property values and rents leads inevitably to massive displacement. During the 1980s, several Harlem churches took the initiative to build low-income housing units for working poor families. Harlem Congregations for Community Development and the now defunct Harlem Development Corporation created 1800 low-income housing units in city-owned buildings. Abyssinian Development Corporation, a project launched by Abyssinian Baptist Church under pastor Calvin O. Butts, also initially built low-income housing, although now ADC's primary investments are in building up the commercial strip on 125th Street and attracting corporate interests. The city has become even less interested in the problem of housing the poor and low wage working-class families. New York City's Housing Preservation Department (HPD) devotes much of its energy to encouraging and supporting high-income buyers. Ibo Balton, HPD director of Manhattan Planning, says that he envisions a process where young African Americans "who went to Yale can buy into Harlem."[8]

Harlem *has* attracted young black Yale graduates and other members of the rising black bourgeoisie. It is also attracting white settlers (the most famous being former President Bill Clinton), though you wouldn't know it from Attie's photos. Not one single white face appears in this community portrait, and for good reason. She set her sights on capturing the old Harlem before it completely disappears, the Harlem that will become our next nostalgic memory, our future golden age. Nevertheless, Harlem's paler settlers are very much part of the story, for they have put a completely different spin on "white flight." Fleeing the more expensive parts of Manhattan, whites are integrating Harlem in large numbers. Unlike the integration of African Americans into white neighborhoods, where fear of declining property values compels white residents to fight (burning crosses, burning houses, mob violence) or flee altogether, whites moving into black communities tend to push property values up, thus pricing many longtime black residents

Minton's Playhouse, the defunct jazz club in the old Hotel Cecil where bebop was allegedly born. The resurrection of Minton's is being made possible under the entrepreneurial hand of Robert DeNiro (whose recent efforts to buy up Harlem deserve their own essay). Even in its most official form, Harlem pride is always black. The MTA's renovation of Harlem subway stations highlight colorful mosaics depicting historic figures such as Marcus Garvey and Thelonious Monk. Busloads of European and Japanese visitors flock to local churches on Sunday mornings and jazz clubs on Saturday nights, all in search of that authentic black experience. Ironically, the very conditions that facilitated tourism have contributed to the slow disappearance of the black working-class culture they seek. Recently, the owner of the Lenox Lounge on Malcolm X Boulevard complained about the lack of local patronage and observed that the tourists were "very disappointed because they are coming for our culture. . . . They want to see how we pop our fingers and get with it, and they get in here, look around, and its nothing but white folks."[16]

LAST DAYS, LAST DAYS, LAST DAYS?

Attie finds death everywhere in Harlem. The most striking thing about her shot of the Home Style Laundromat is the makeshift memorial of flowers perched on top of a huge "box" of sorts. Underneath the flowers someone scrawled "Crips," the name of a notorious gang, in white spray paint. Standing in the entrance of the laundromat is an African, perhaps the owner or an employee? What or who is dying here? Was someone shot? Is the business dying? Does this image represent the death of the old African-American and Caribbean Harlem and the birth of a new, West African Harlem? After all, New York is now home to well over 100,000 Africans, mostly from Mali, Senegal, Ghana, Somalia, Nigeria, and the Congo, and a large proportion of these residents are concentrated around 116th Street.[17] Attie unearths several other street memorials, the majority of which are works by aerosol artists and probably no longer exist. And they can all serve as commentary on the death of old Harlem as well as memorials for the individuals for whom they were created. One of these, "RIP Chino Chan," describes the deceased as having "entered the realm of legends but will be missed by your past . . . it is time to start a new path." Another aerosol work consists of a sweet poem on a scroll framed by a most striking silhouette of tombstones against a midnight blue background that resemble the New York's skyline. A particularly powerful and telling piece consists of a careful rendering of "Buster," the deceased, in spray paint and a long, moving poem, part of which reads, "I can keep this poem going for days, with plenty/ things to say. But you will be in my heart and stay/ in my mind, every single day. From 125 and 124/ Lenox Ave. Your body will be gone But the/ Ave. will always miss you." But over this poem, on the orange storefront security gate is a message quickly scribbled in dripping white spray paint, "Moved to 1972 7th Ave., bet. 118 and 119." Here we witness two deaths superimposed on one another.

So many of the buildings Attie captured feel like they are waiting to die, or waiting for a hurricane. Consider the White Cross Shoe Clinic, where beneath its large black and white sign, someone wrote "Last Days, Last Days, Last Days" over the top of the graffiti-tagged green security gate. It is a clear and legible sign of what is to come. Or is it? I cannot help but think of the irony of a place called "White Cross" signaling the death of Harlem when some eighty years ago, Marcus Garvey's Black Cross Nurses marched along these very streets with a mission of community uplift. The Black Cross nurses, an auxiliary of the Universal Negro Improvement Association (UNIA), instilled black people with racial pride and ministered to the needs of black men, some dressed on military regalia in preparation for war with white supremacy. The UNIA (whose Harlem branch was the largest single branch in the world) preached entrepreneurship and black ownership of property and business in Harlem.[18] Yet, even in this seemingly isolated shot of a dying street, Garvey's Ghost rears his head in the form of a small poster positioned to the left of the façade: "Stand Up for Mumia."

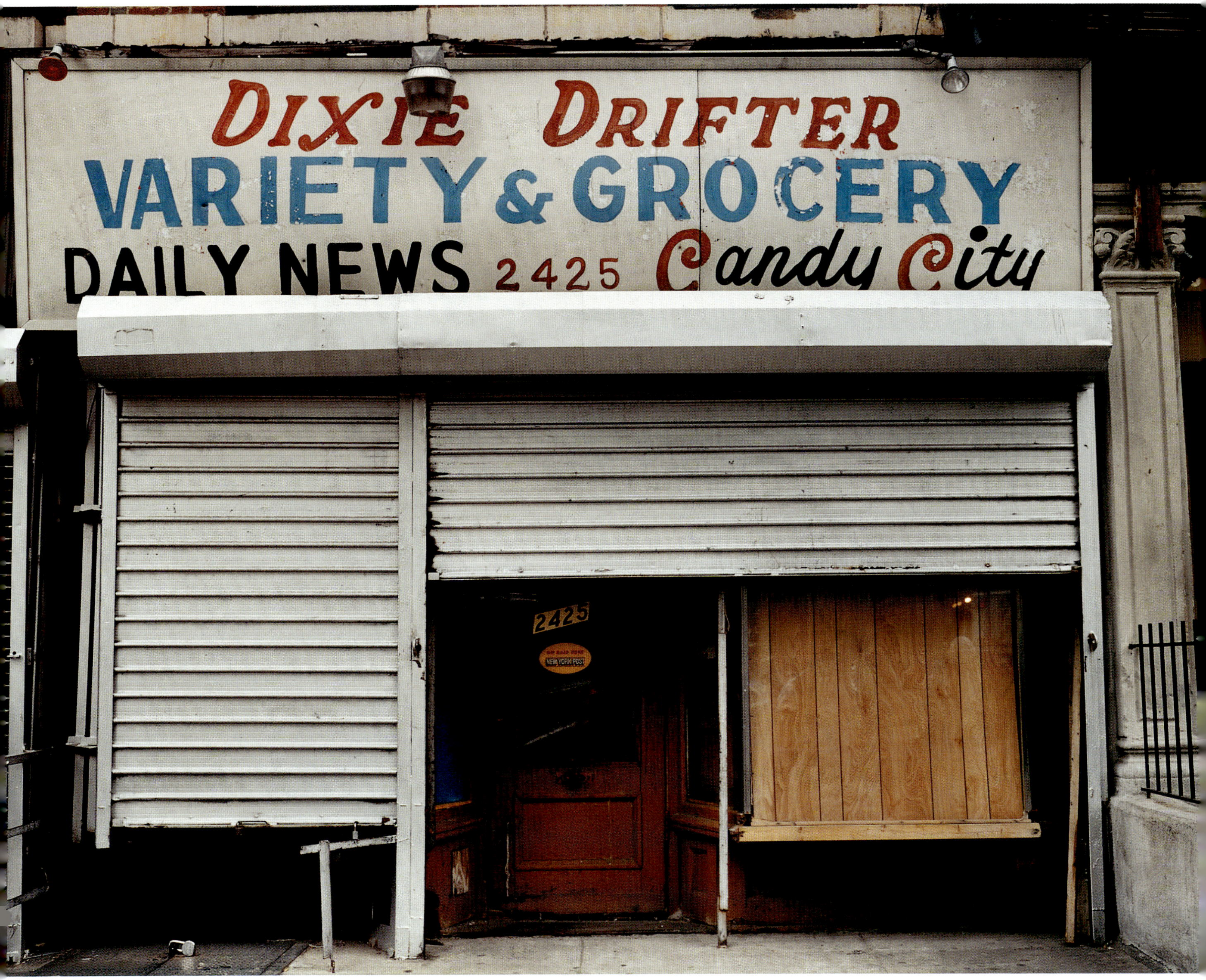
DIXIE DRIFTER
VARIETY & GROCERY
DAILY NEWS 2425 Candy City
2425
NEW YORK POST

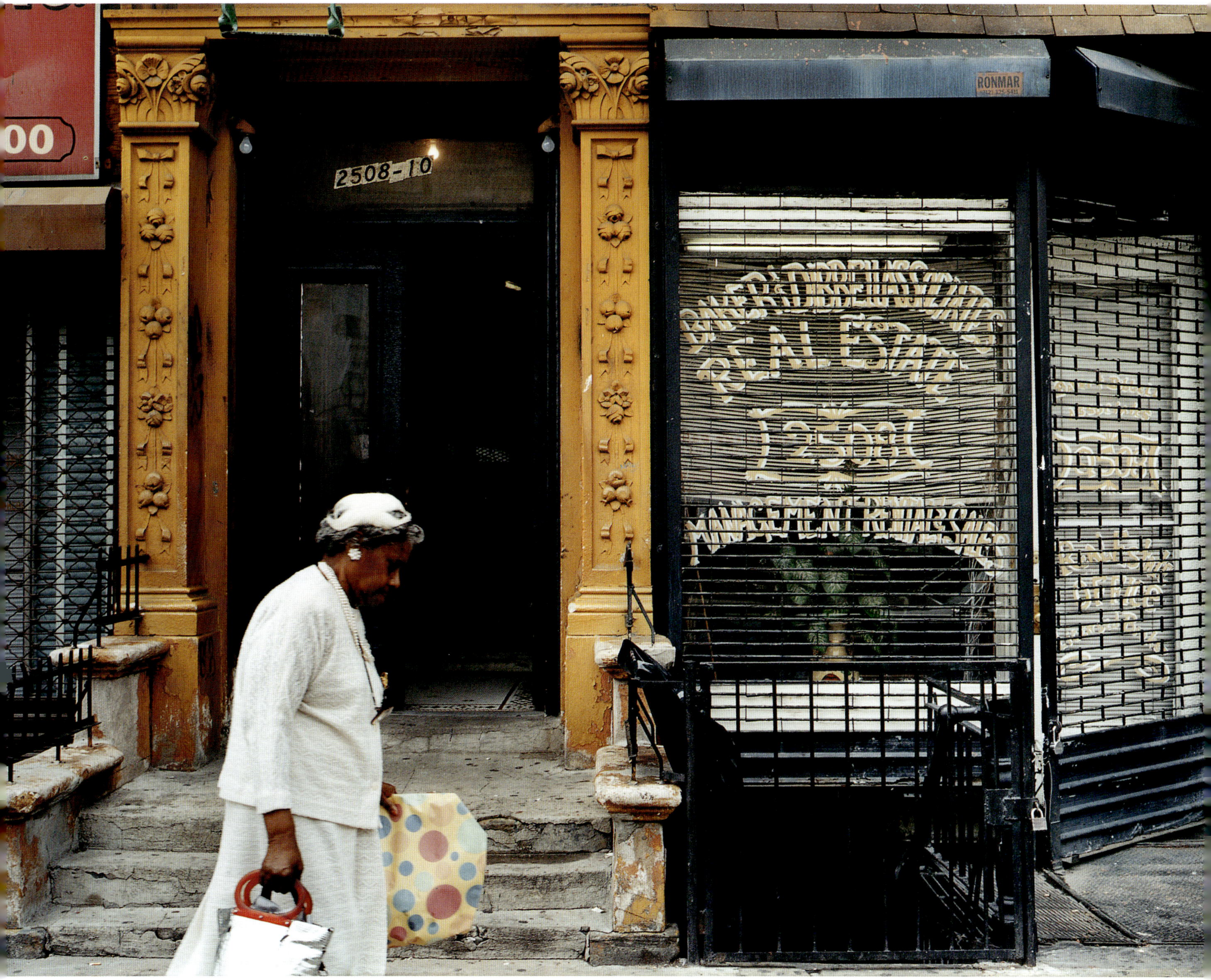
2508-10
RONMAR

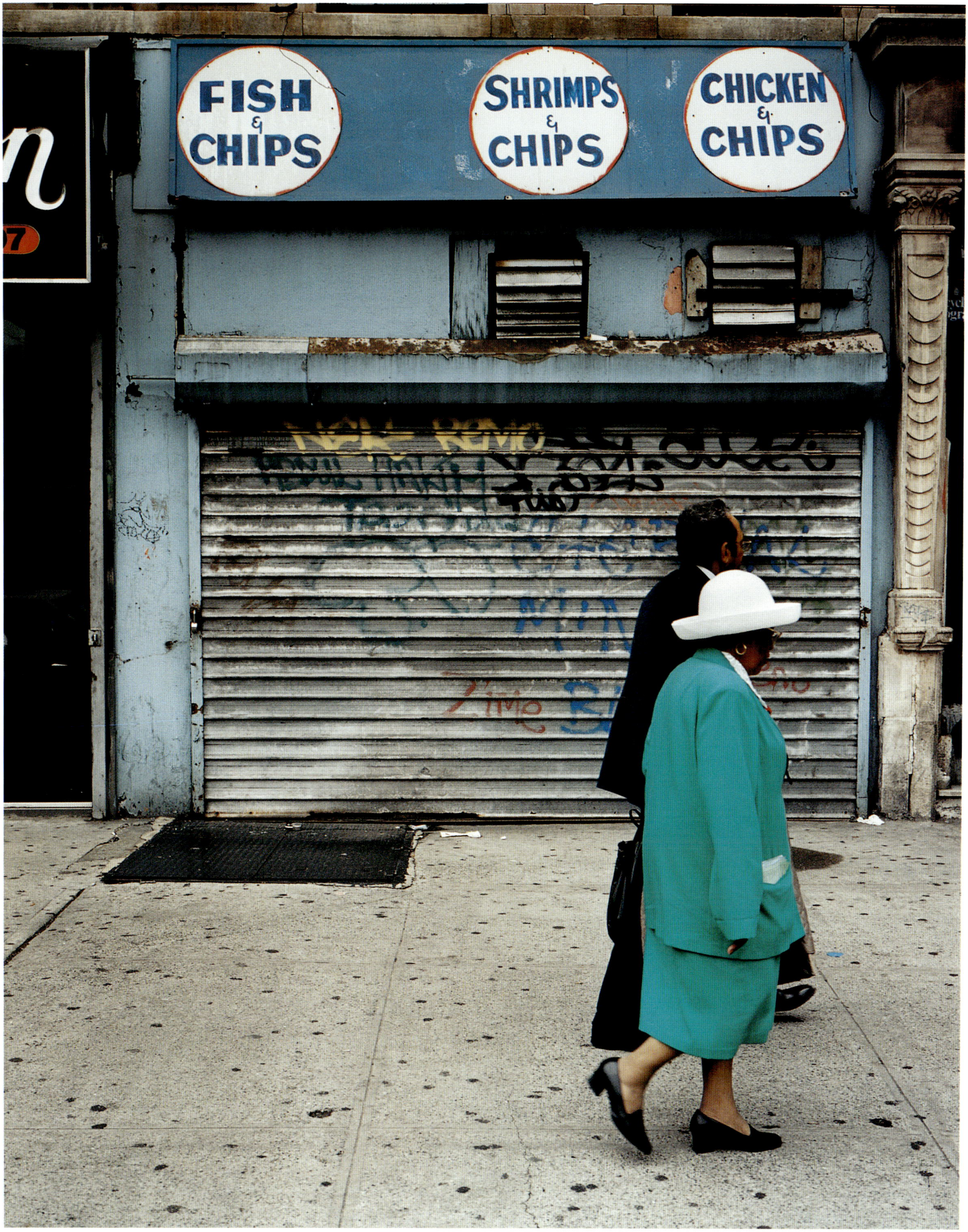
FISH & CHIPS
SHRIMPS & CHIPS
CHICKEN & CHIPS

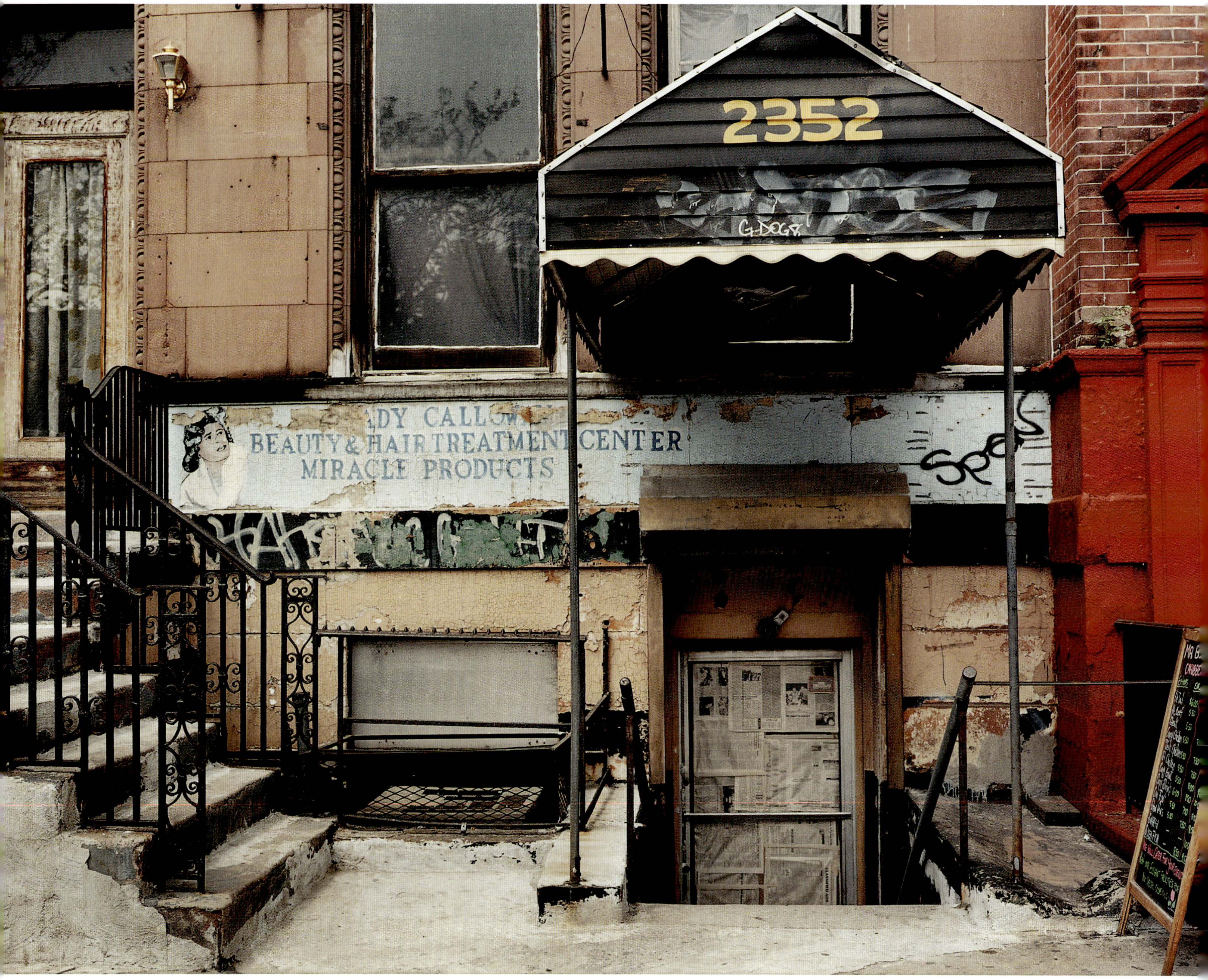
2352
ADY CALLOW
BEAUTY & HAIR TREATMENT CENTER
MIRACLE PRODUCTS

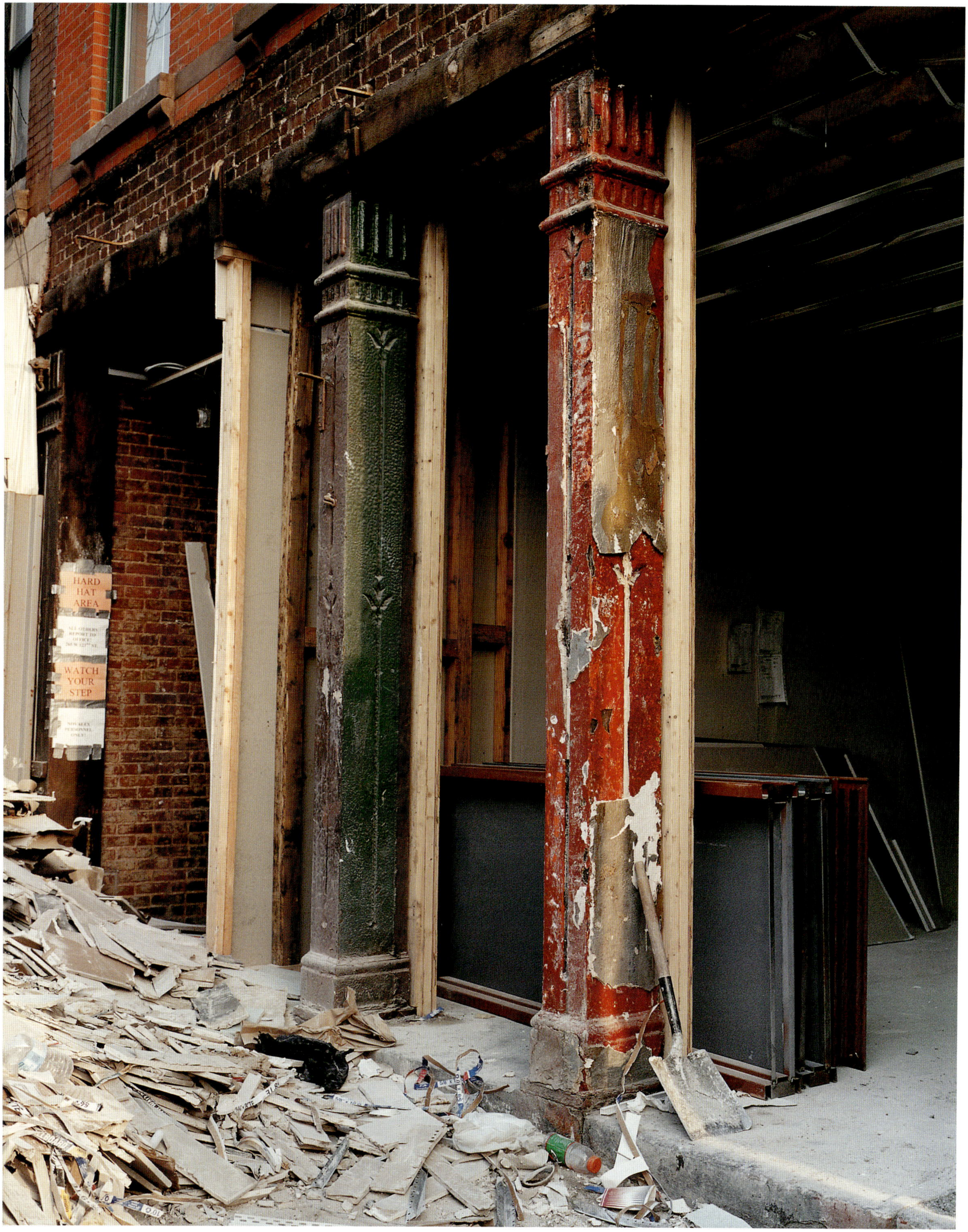
HARD HAT AREA
WATCH YOUR STEP

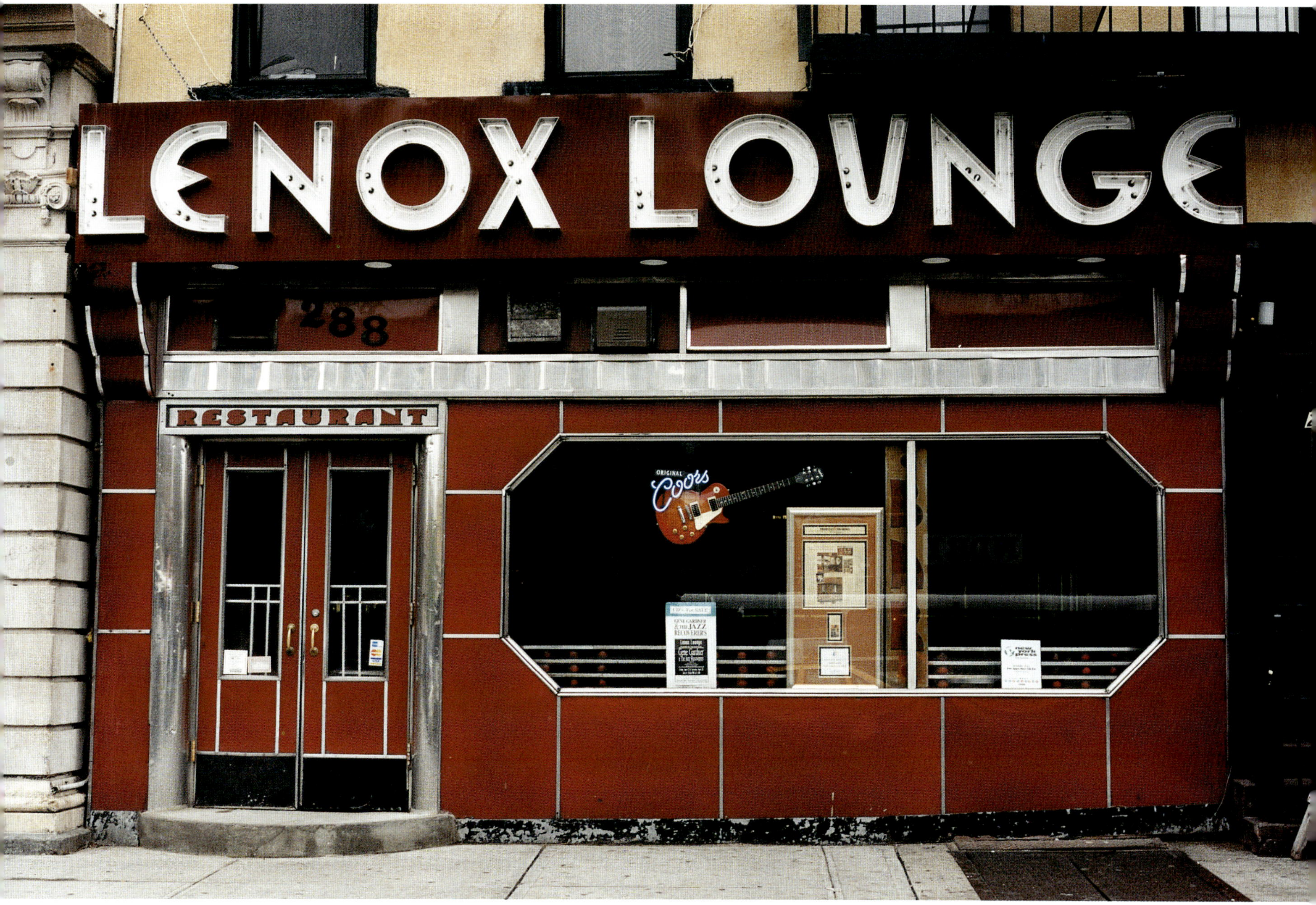
LENOX LOUNGE
288
RESTAURANT
ORIGINAL
Coors

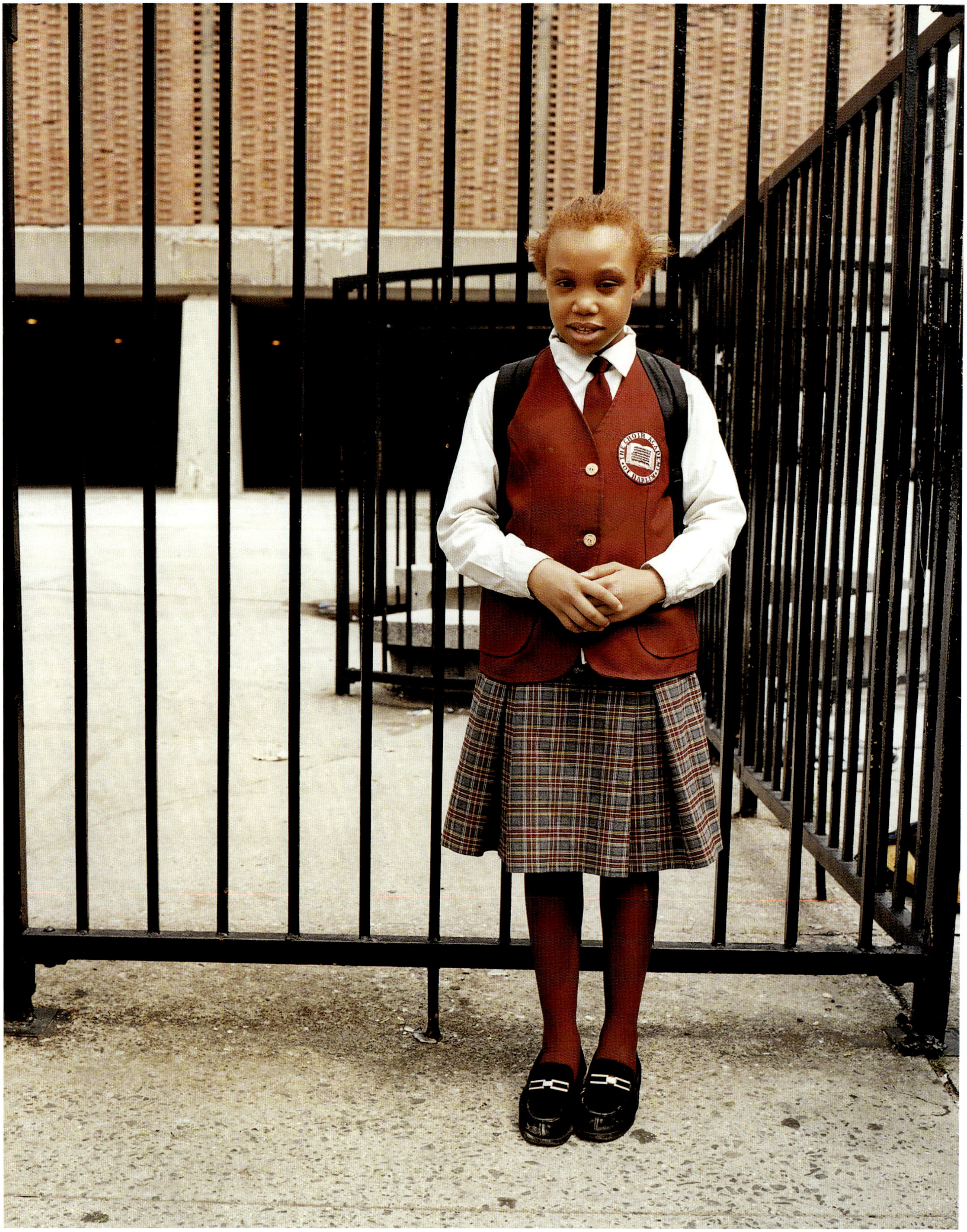
THE CHOIR ACADEMY
OF HARLEM

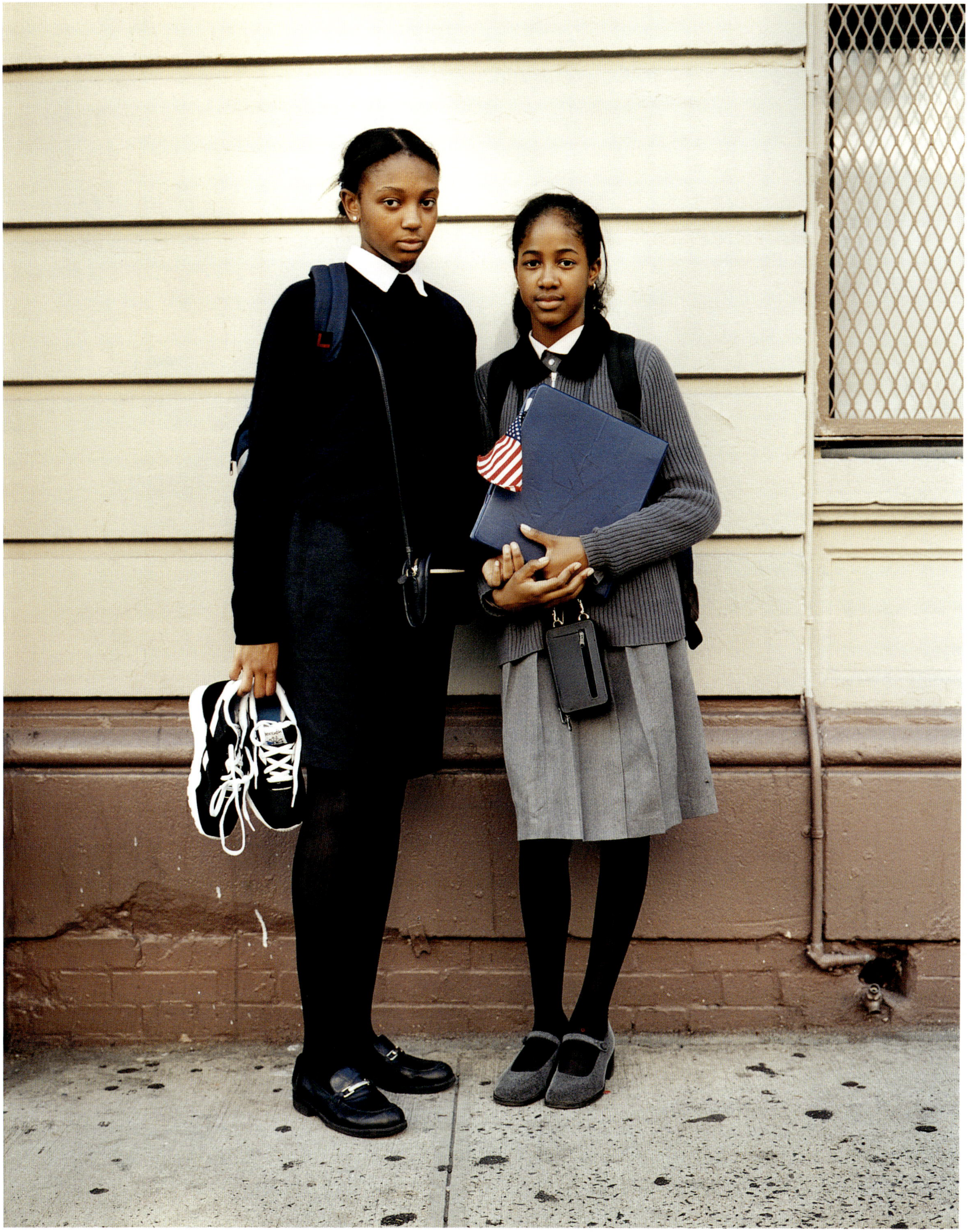

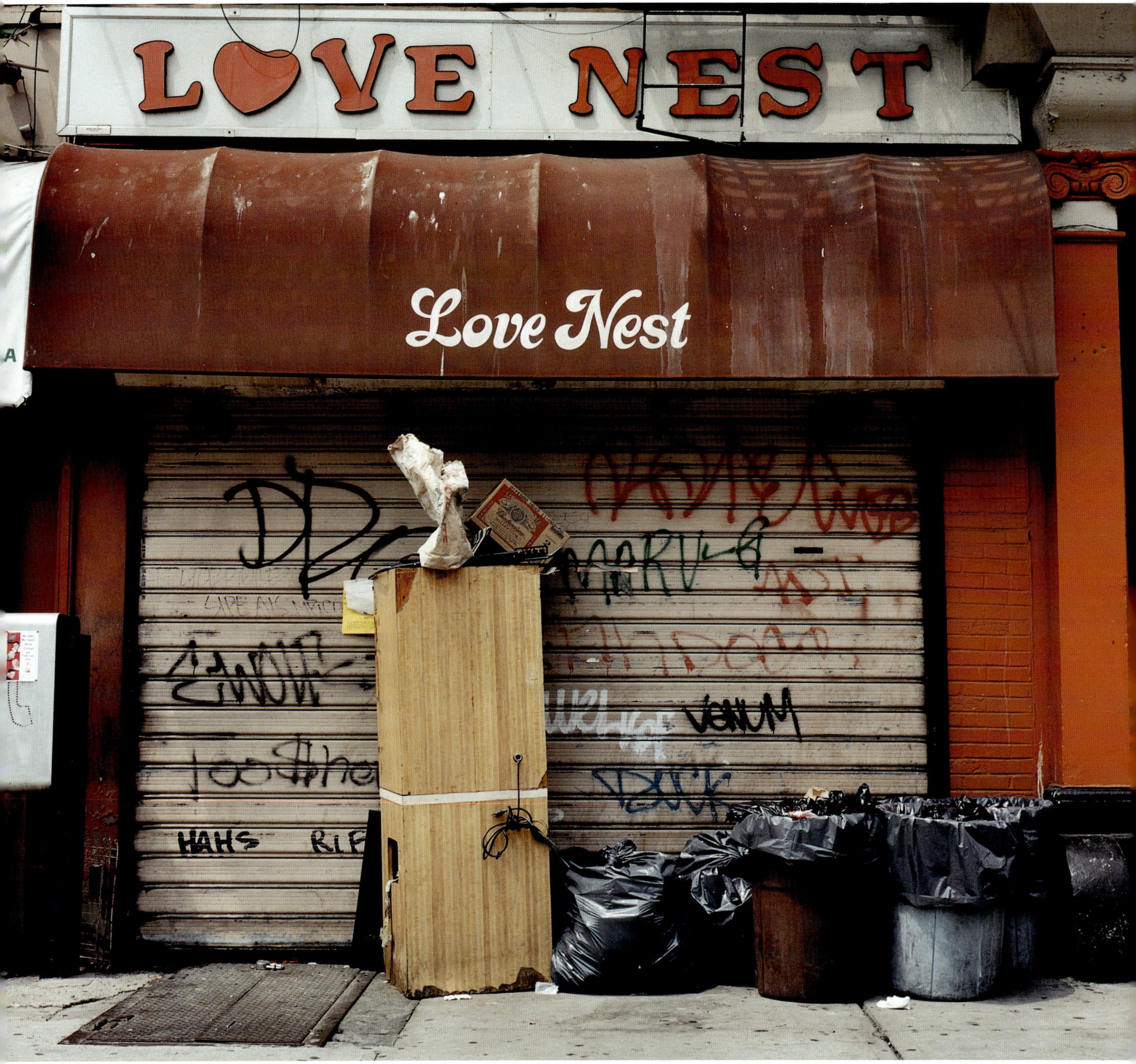
LOVE NEST
Love Nest
VENUM

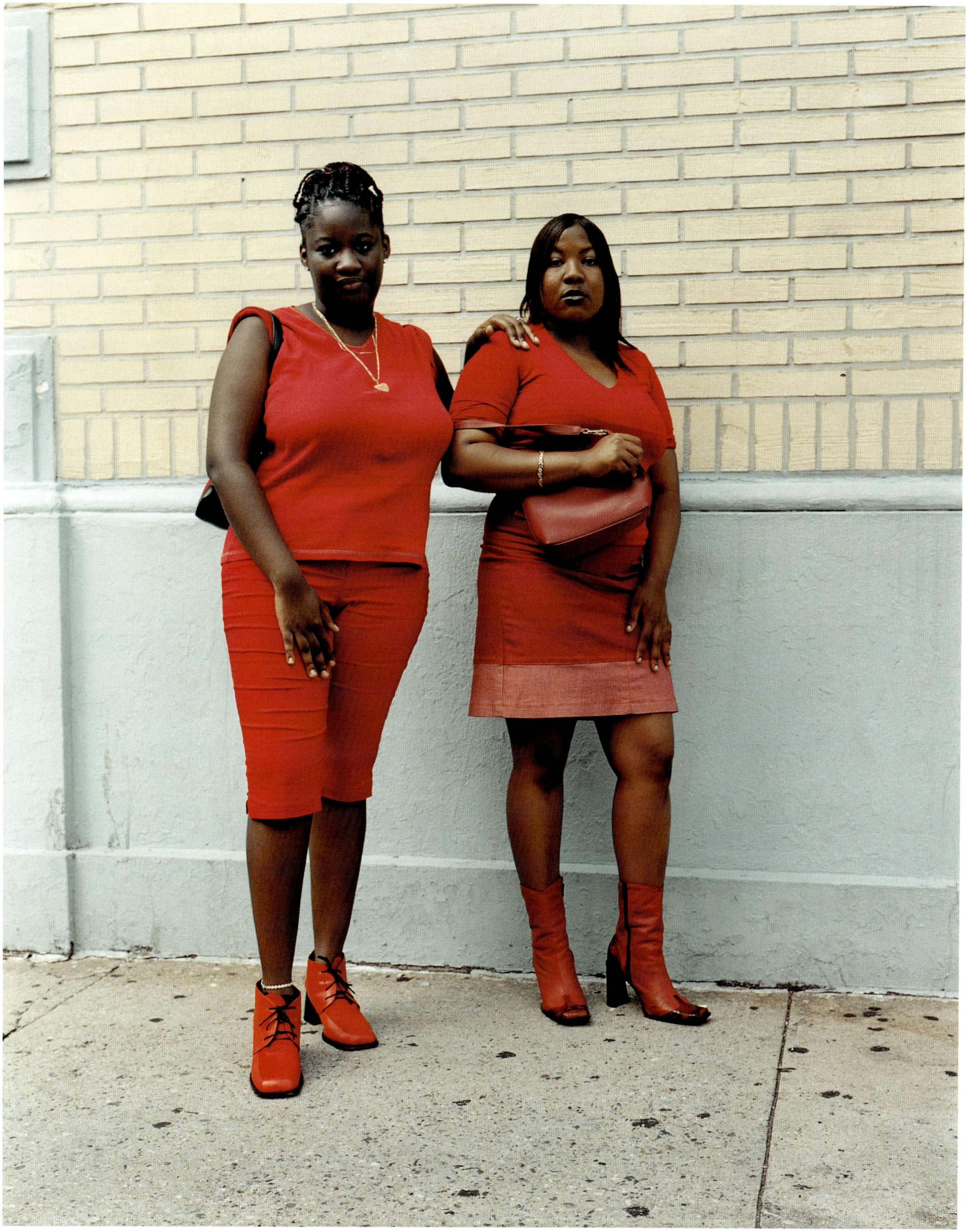

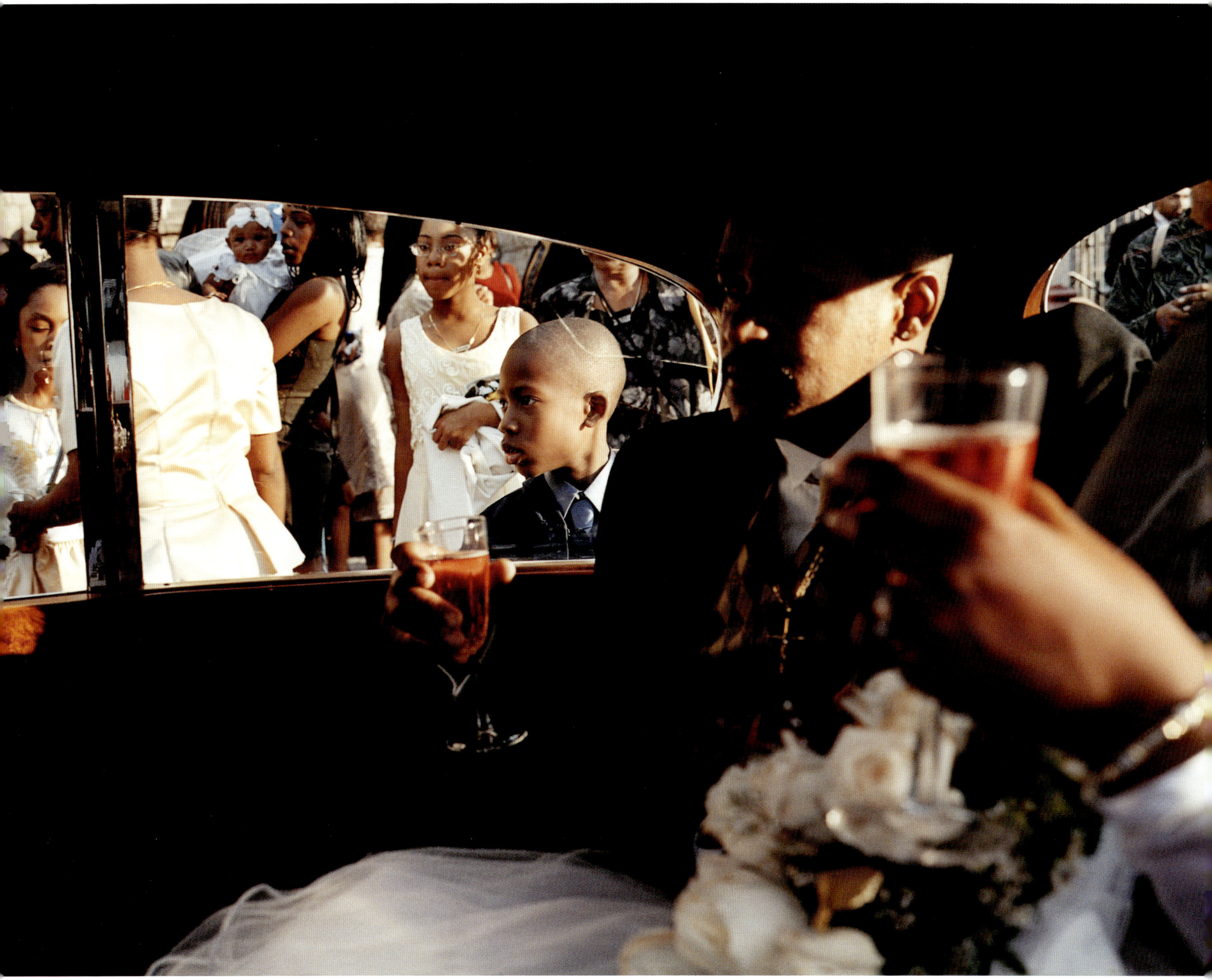

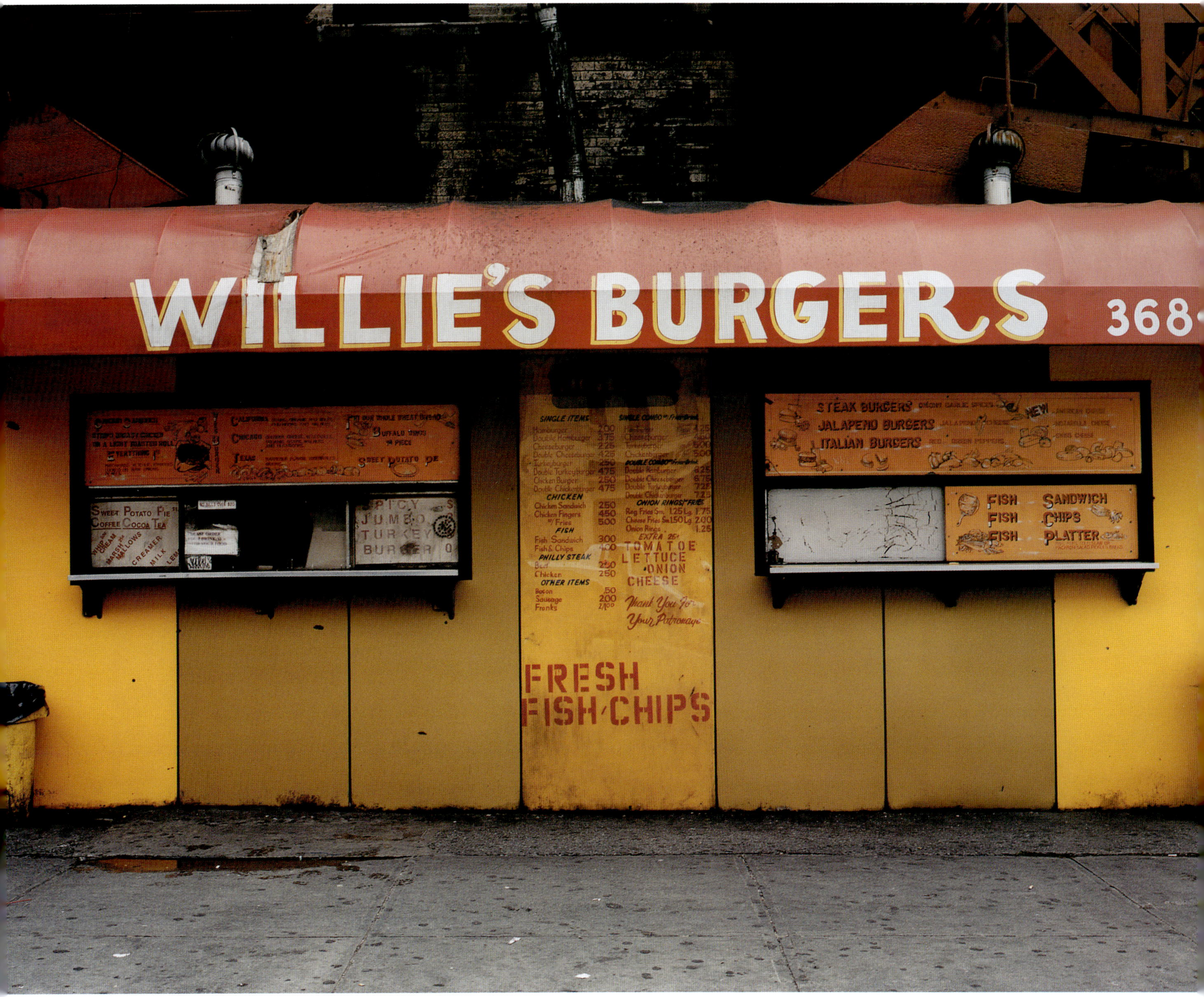
WILLIE'S BURGERS
368
STEAK BURGERS
JALAPENO BURGERS
ITALIAN BURGERS
NEW
FISH SANDWICH
FISH CHIPS
FISH PLATTER
SWEET POTATO PIE
COFFEE COCOA TEA
SPICY JUMBO TURKEY BURGER
TOMATOE
LETTUCE
ONION
CHEESE
Thank You For Your Patronage
FRESH
FISH CHIPS

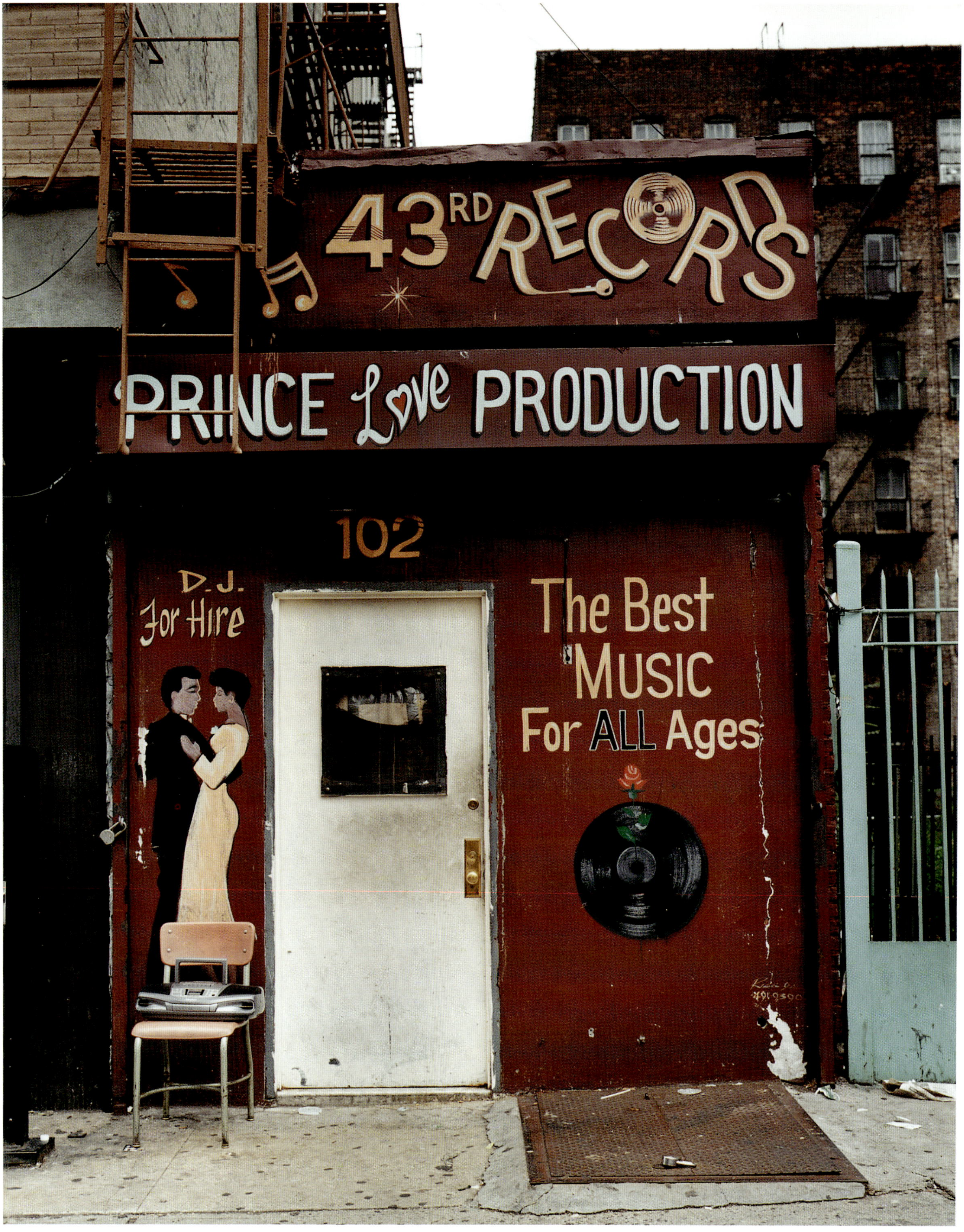
43RD RECORDS
PRINCE Love PRODUCTION
102
D.J.
For Hire
The Best
MUSIC
For ALL Ages

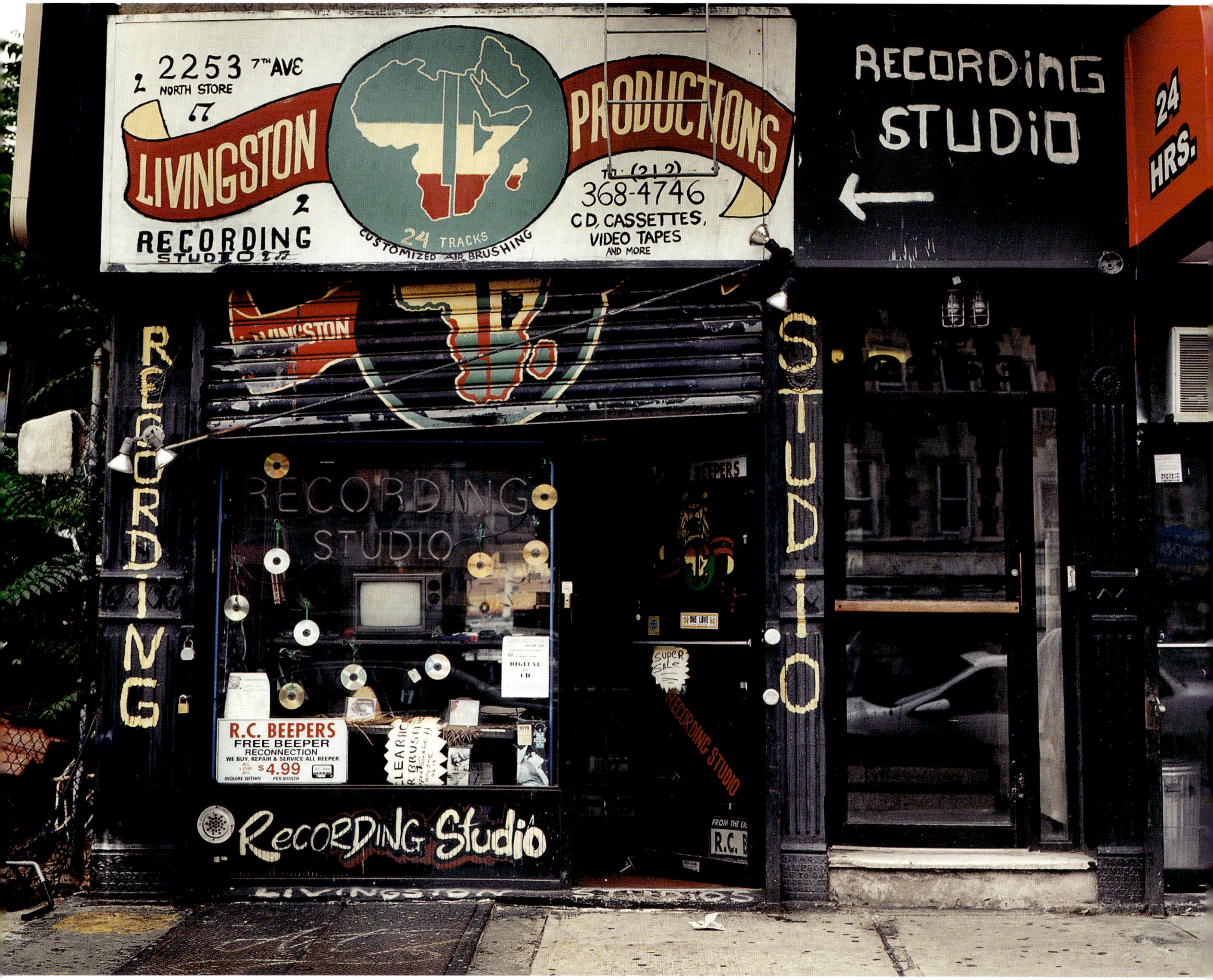
2253 7TH AVE
NORTH STORE
LIVINGSTON
PRODUCTIONS
RECORDING
STUDIO
24 TRACKS
CUSTOMIZED AIR BRUSHING
TEL (212)
368-4746
CD, CASSETTES,
VIDEO TAPES
AND MORE
RECORDING
STUDIO
24 HRS.
RECORDING
STUDIO
RECORDING STUDIO
R.C. BEEPERS
FREE BEEPER
RECONNECTION
WE BUY, REPAIR & SERVICE ALL BEEPER
$4.99
Recording Studio
SUPER SALE
RECORDING STUDIO

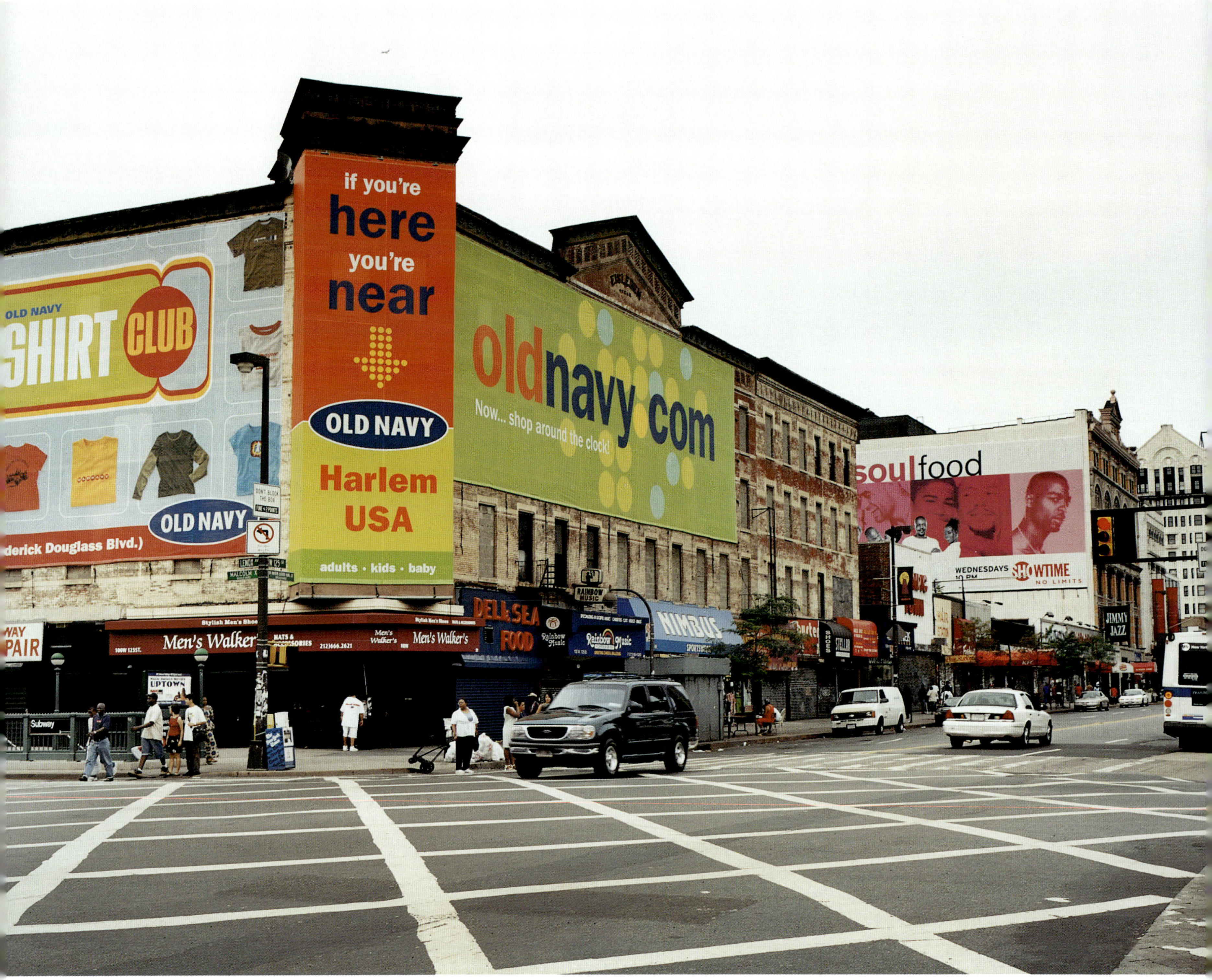
OLD NAVY
SHIRT CLUB
OLD NAVY
derick Douglass Blvd.)
if you're
here
you're
near
OLD NAVY
Harlem
USA
adults • kids • baby
oldnavy.com
Now... shop around the clock!
soulfood
WEDNESDAYS
SHOWTIME
NO LIMITS
Men's Walker
Men's Walker's
DELI & SEA
FOOD
Rainbow Music
NIMBUS
JIMMY JAZZ
UPTOWN
Subway

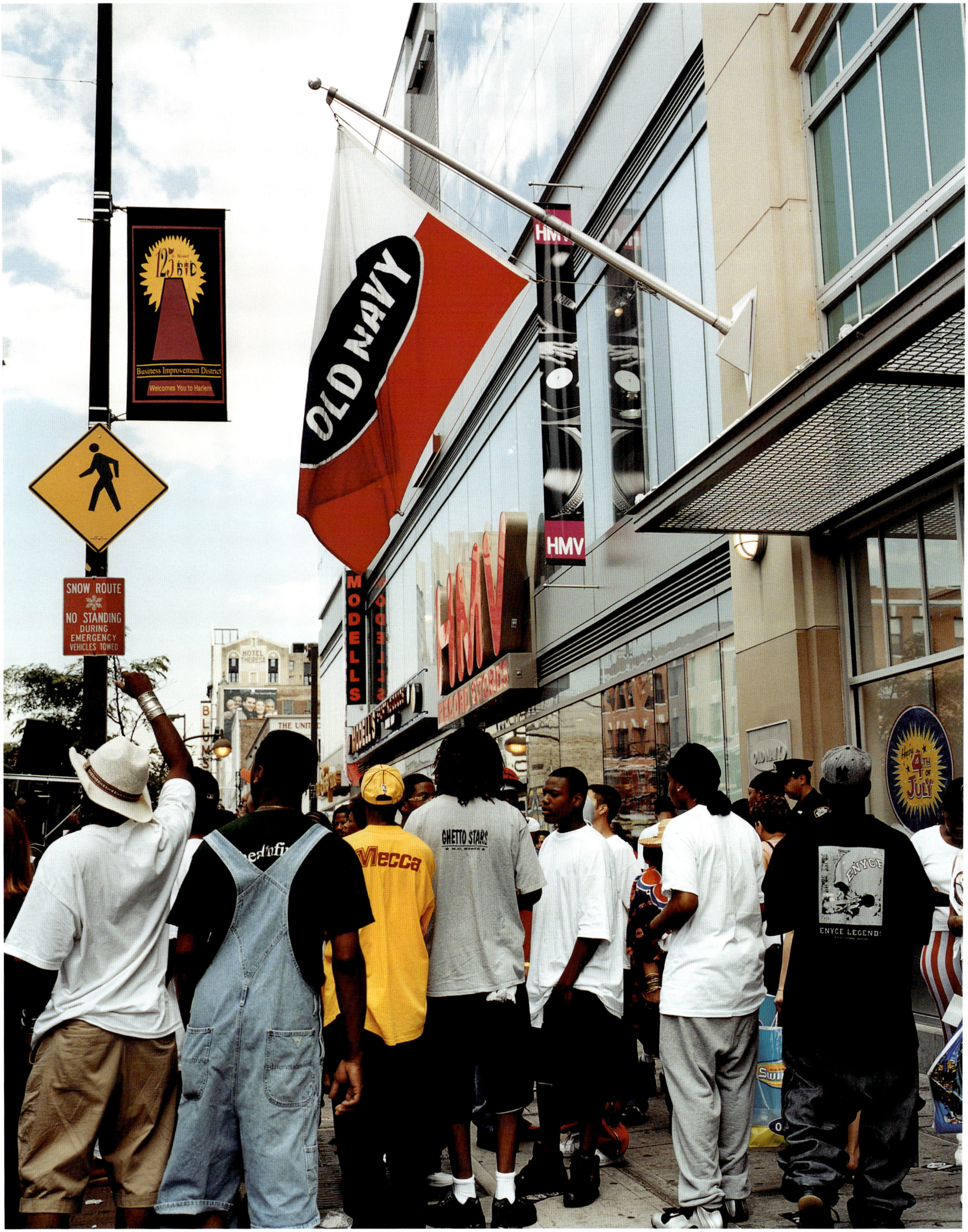

Business Improvement District
Welcomes You to Harlem
SNOW ROUTE
NO STANDING
DURING
EMERGENCY
VEHICLES TOWED
OLD NAVY
HMV
HMV
MODELLS
HMV
RECORD STORES
HOTEL THERESA
GHETTO STARS
Mecca
ENYCE LEGENDS
4TH OF JULY

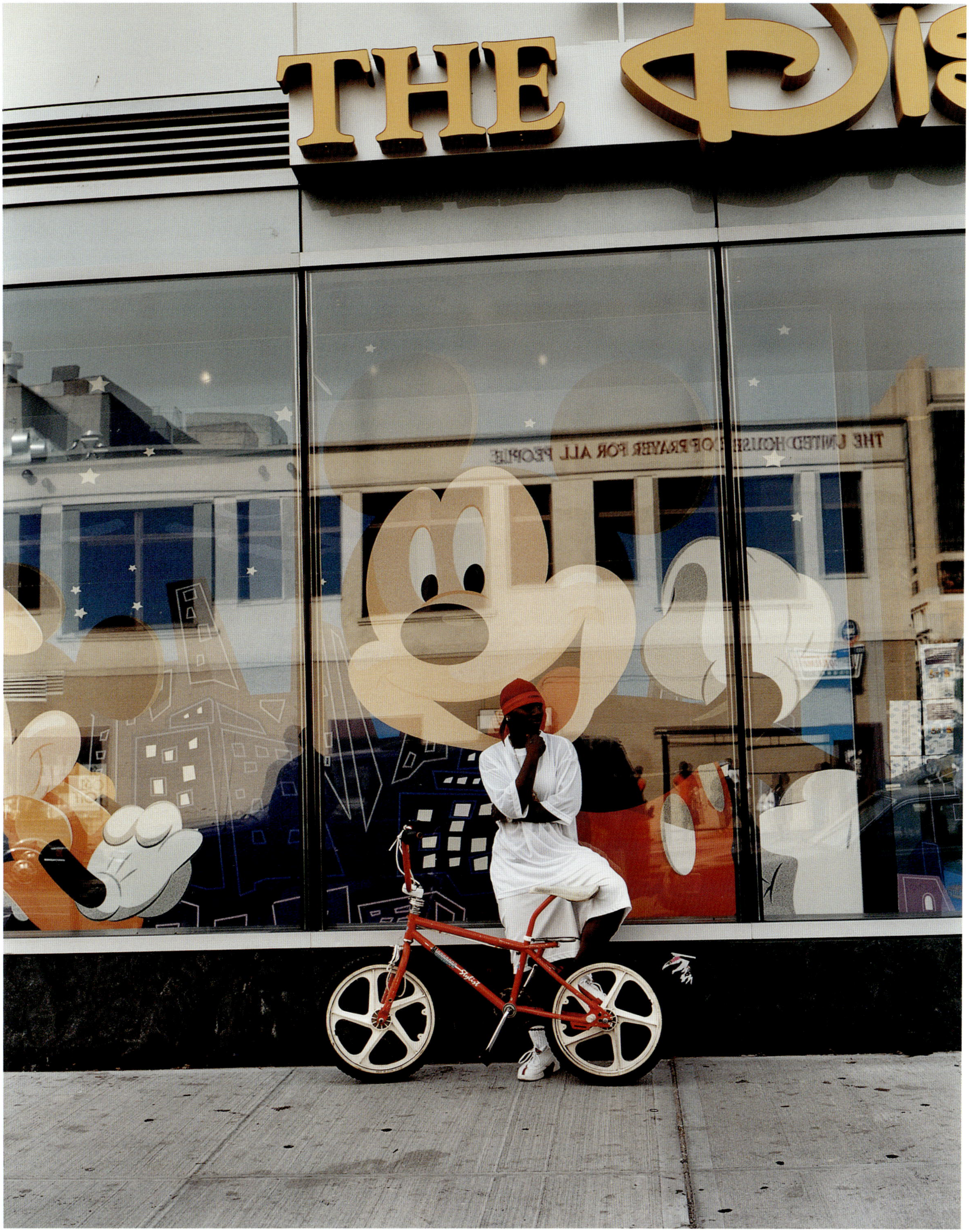
THE

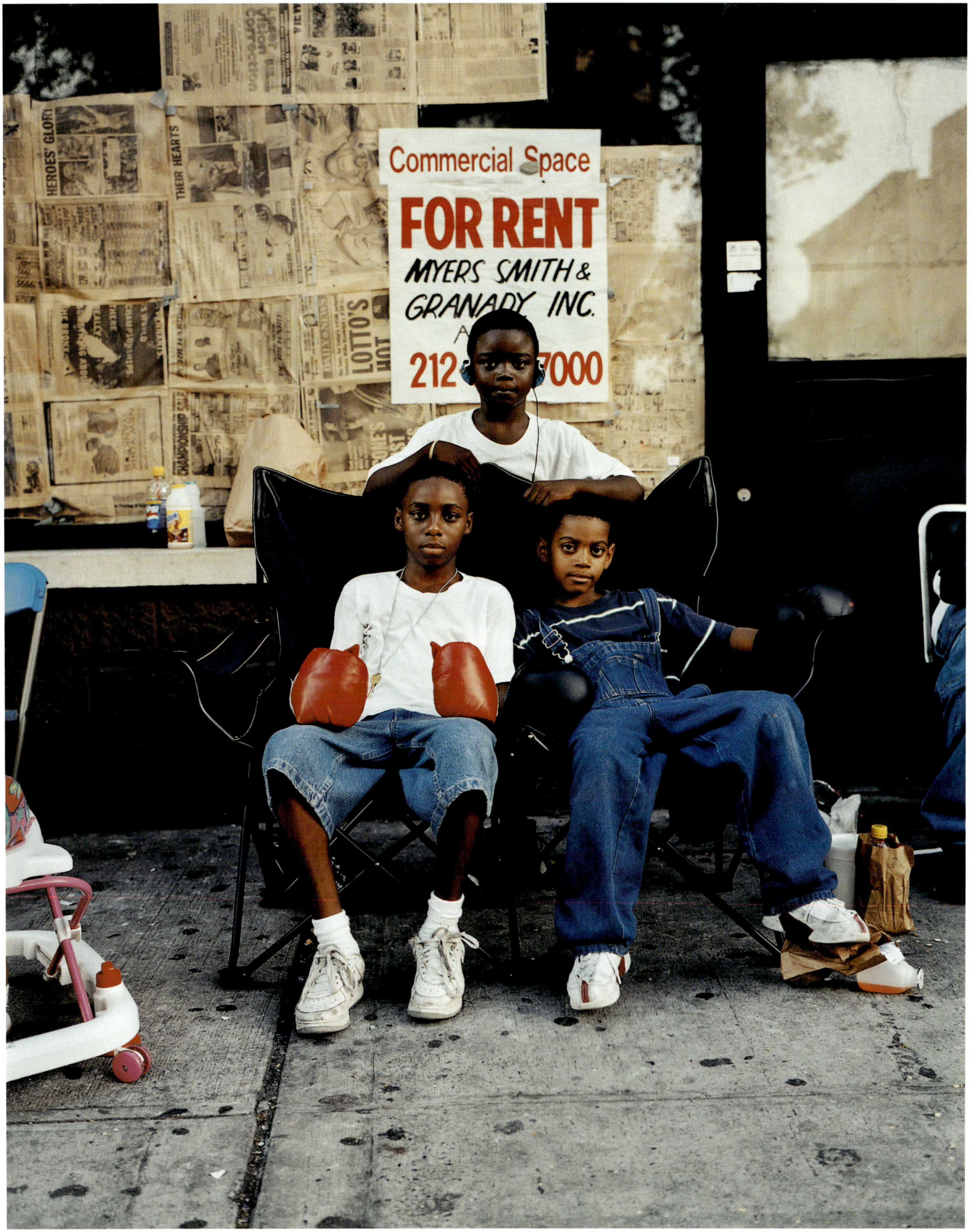
Commercial Space
FOR RENT
MYERS SMITH &
GRANADY INC.
212
7000

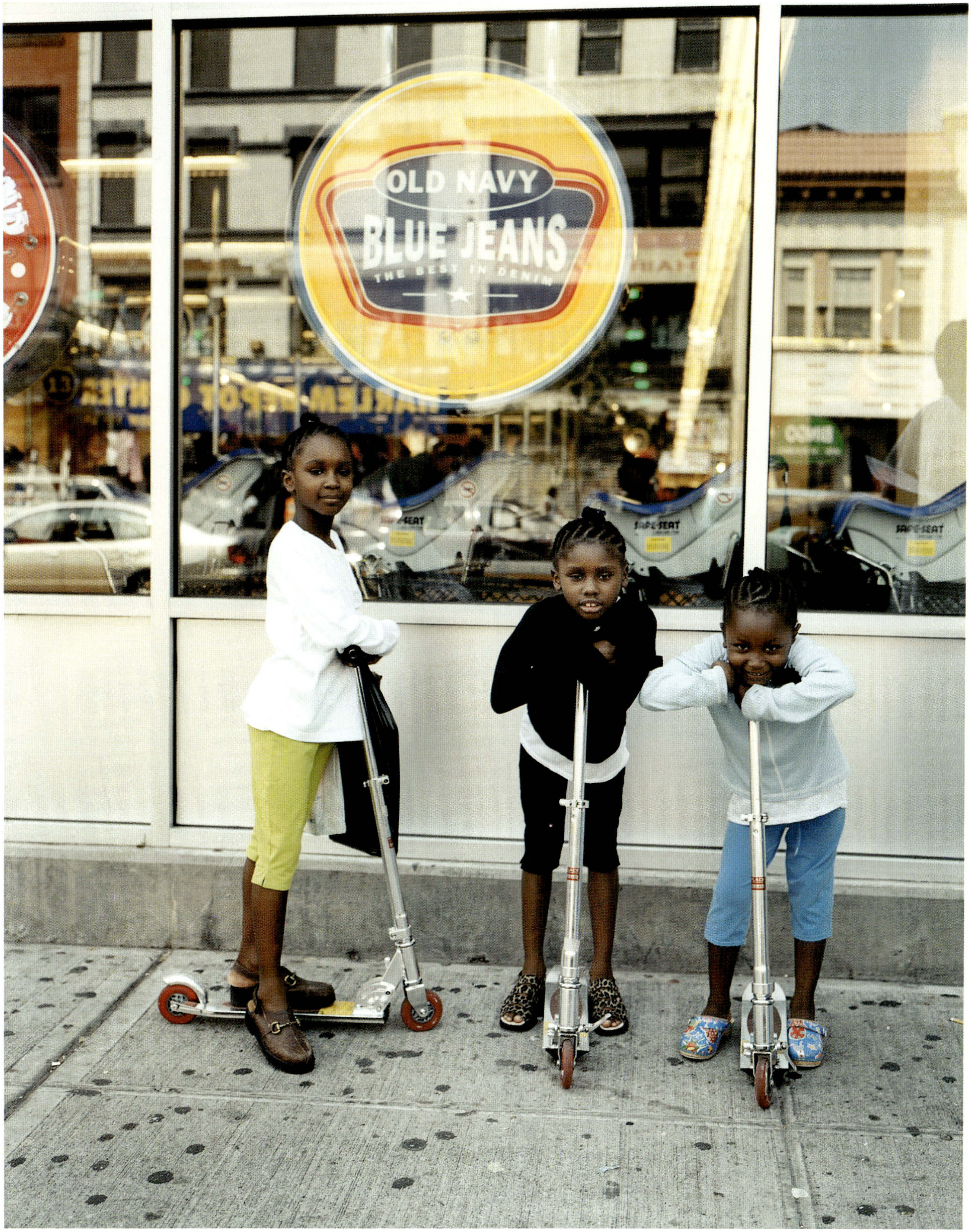
OLD NAVY
BLUE JEANS
THE BEST IN DENIM

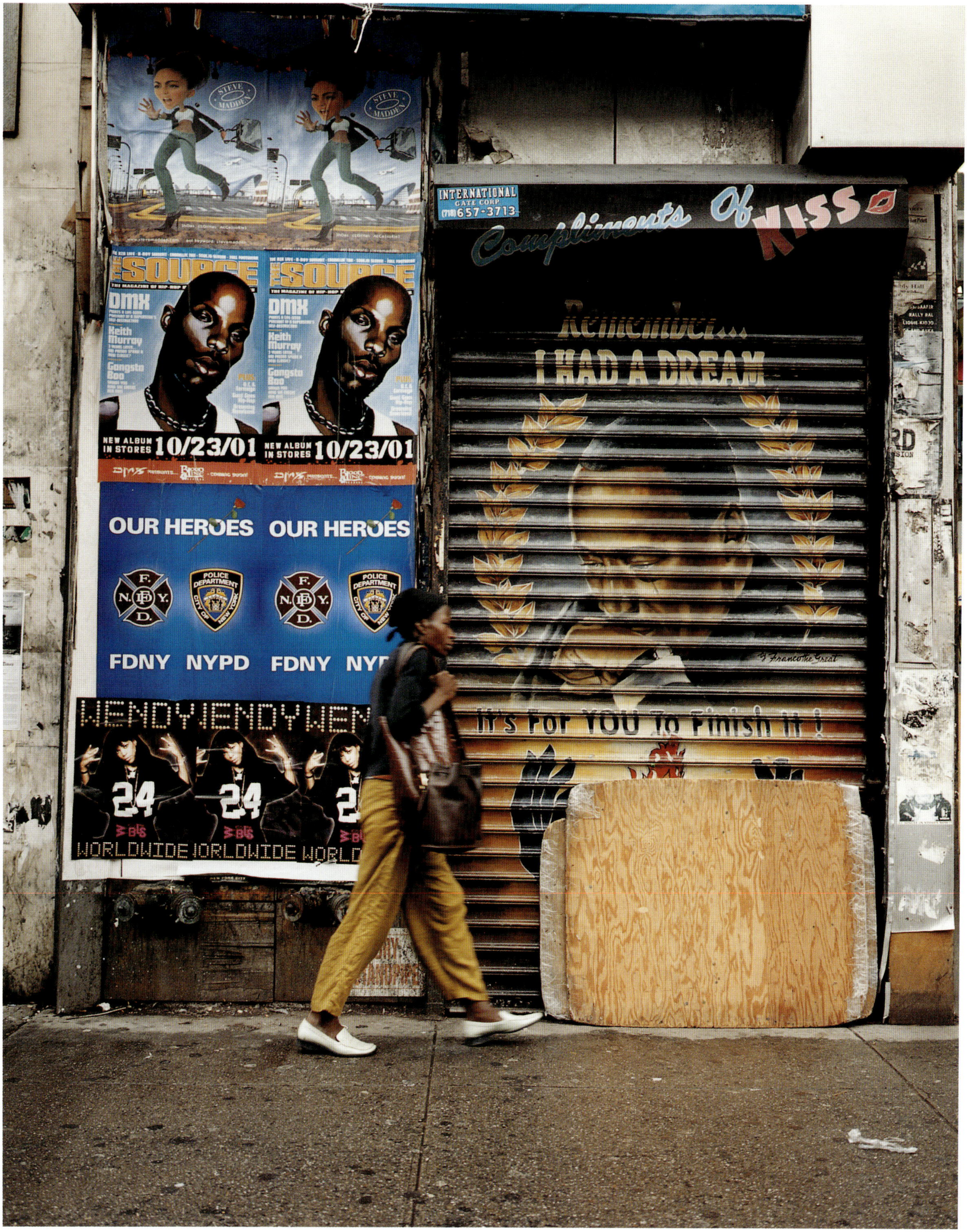
STEVE MADDEN
STEVE MADDEN
THE SOURCE
THE SOURCE
DMX
Keith Murray
Gangsta Boo
DMX
Keith Murray
Gangsta Boo
NEW ALBUM IN STORES 10/23/01
NEW ALBUM IN STORES 10/23/01
OUR HEROES
OUR HEROES
F.D.N.Y.
POLICE DEPARTMENT CITY OF NEW YORK
F.D.N.Y.
POLICE DEPARTMENT CITY OF NEW YORK
FDNY NYPD FDNY NY
WENDYWENDYWEN
24
24
WORLDWIDE WORLDWIDE WORLD
INTERNATIONAL GATE CORP (718) 657-3713
Compliments Of KISS
I HAD A DREAM
It's For YOU To Finish It !

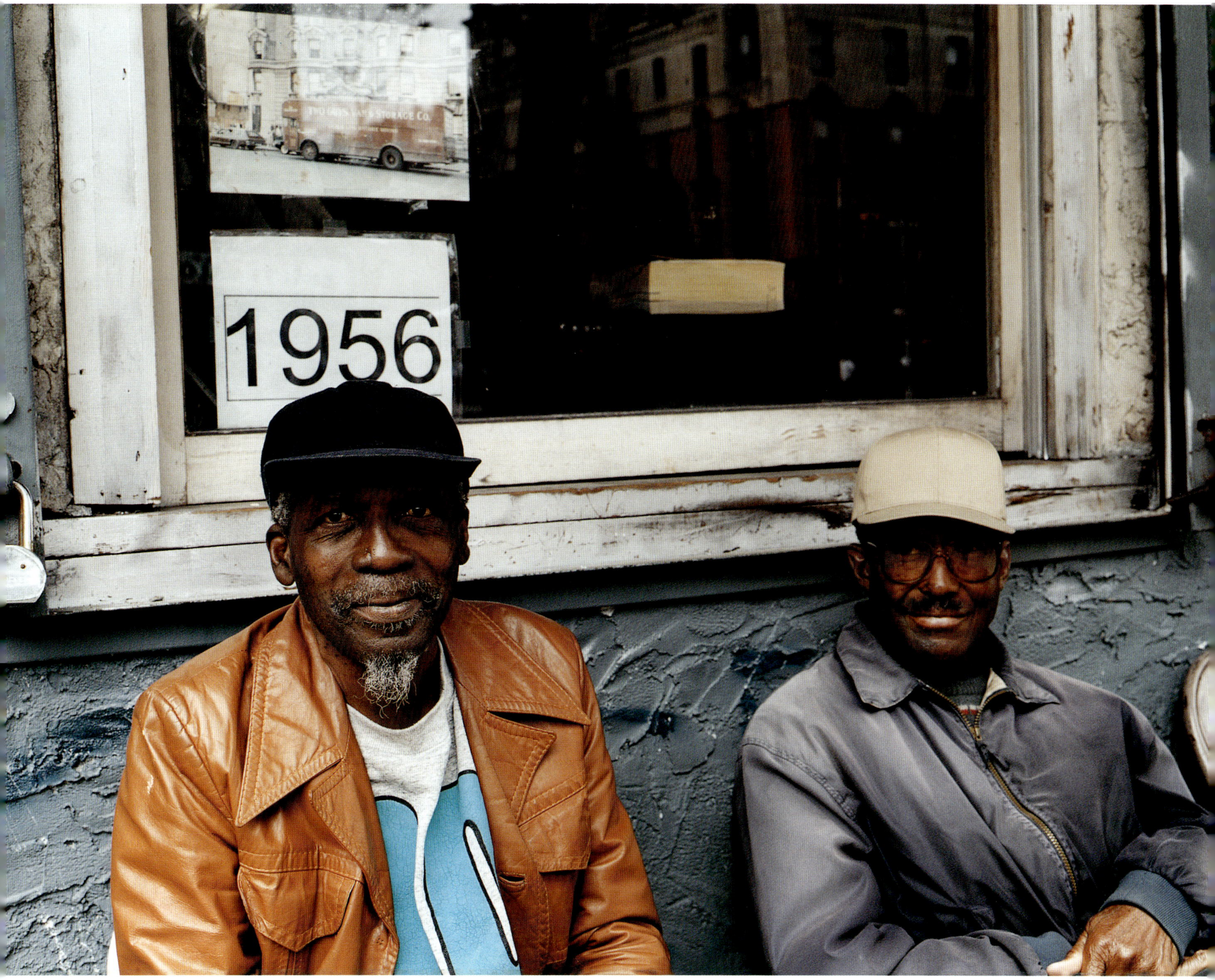
1956

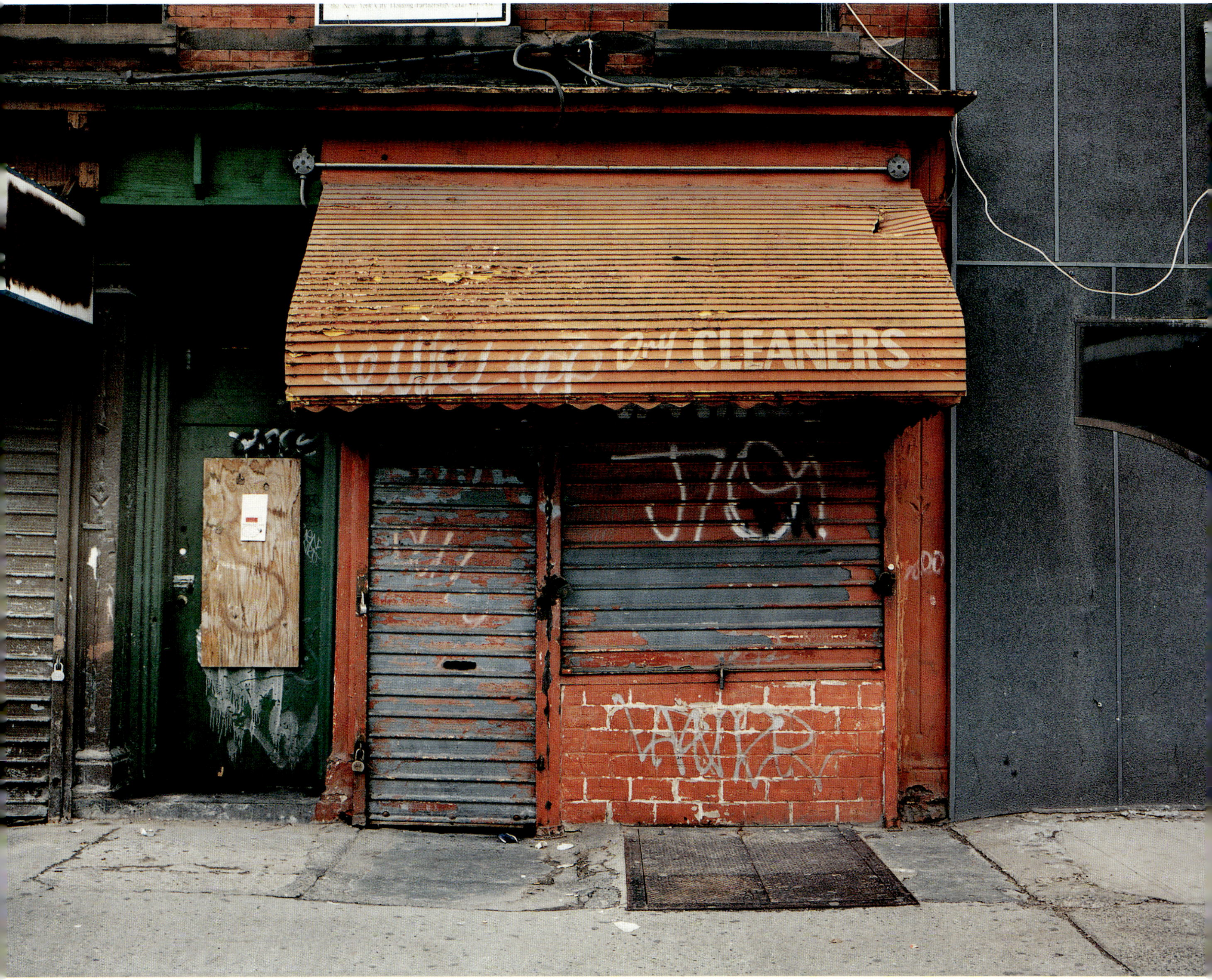
Dry CLEANERS

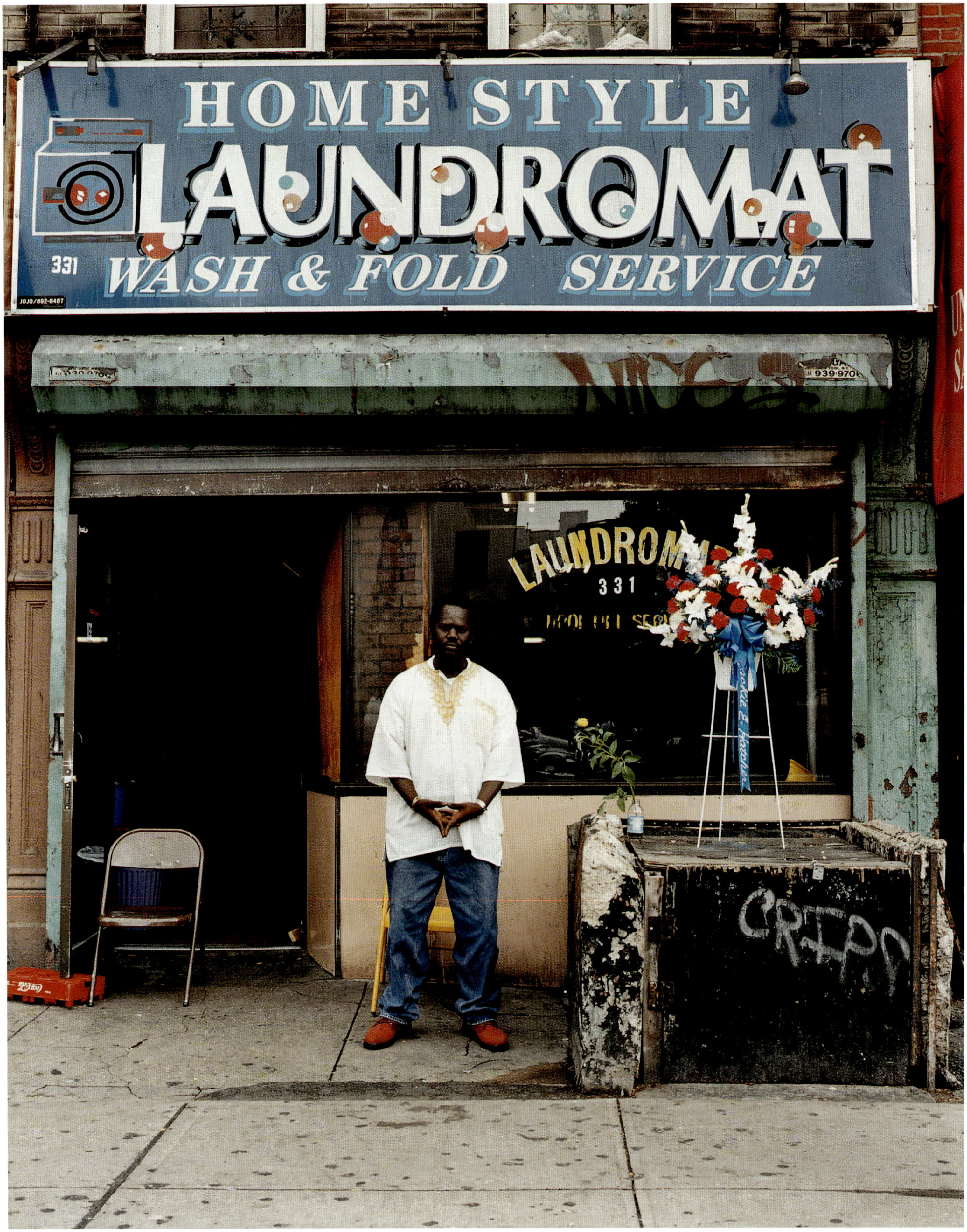
HOME STYLE
LAUNDROMAT
331
WASH & FOLD SERVICE
LAUNDROMAT
331
CRIPS

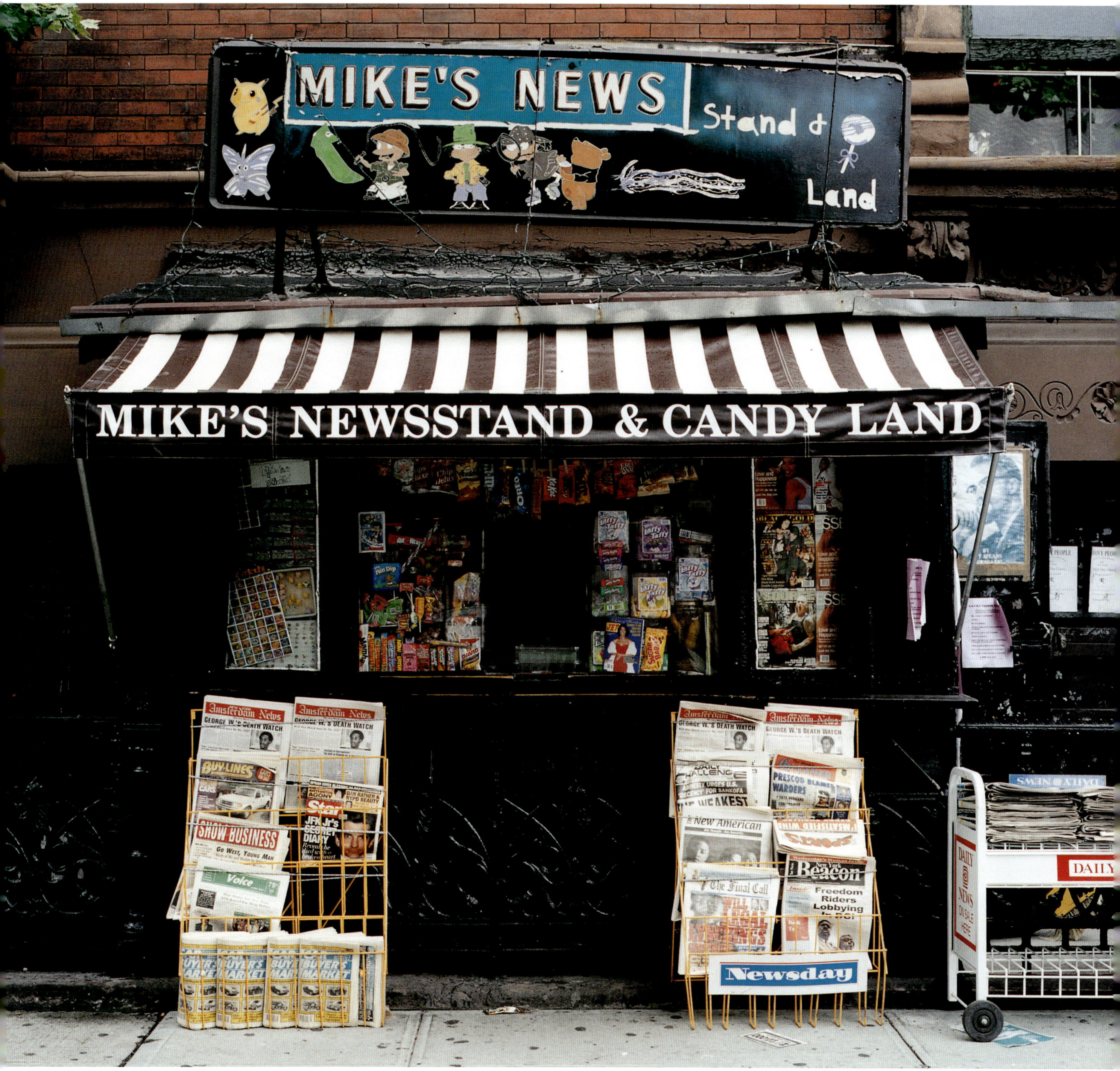
MIKE'S NEWS
Stand &
Land
MIKE'S NEWSSTAND & CANDY LAND
Amsterdam News
GEORGE W.'S DEATH WATCH
SHOW BUSINESS
Go West, Young Man
Voice
Star
JFK Jr's Secret Diary
The New American
Beacon
Freedom Riders Lobbying
The Final Call
Newsday
DAILY NEWS

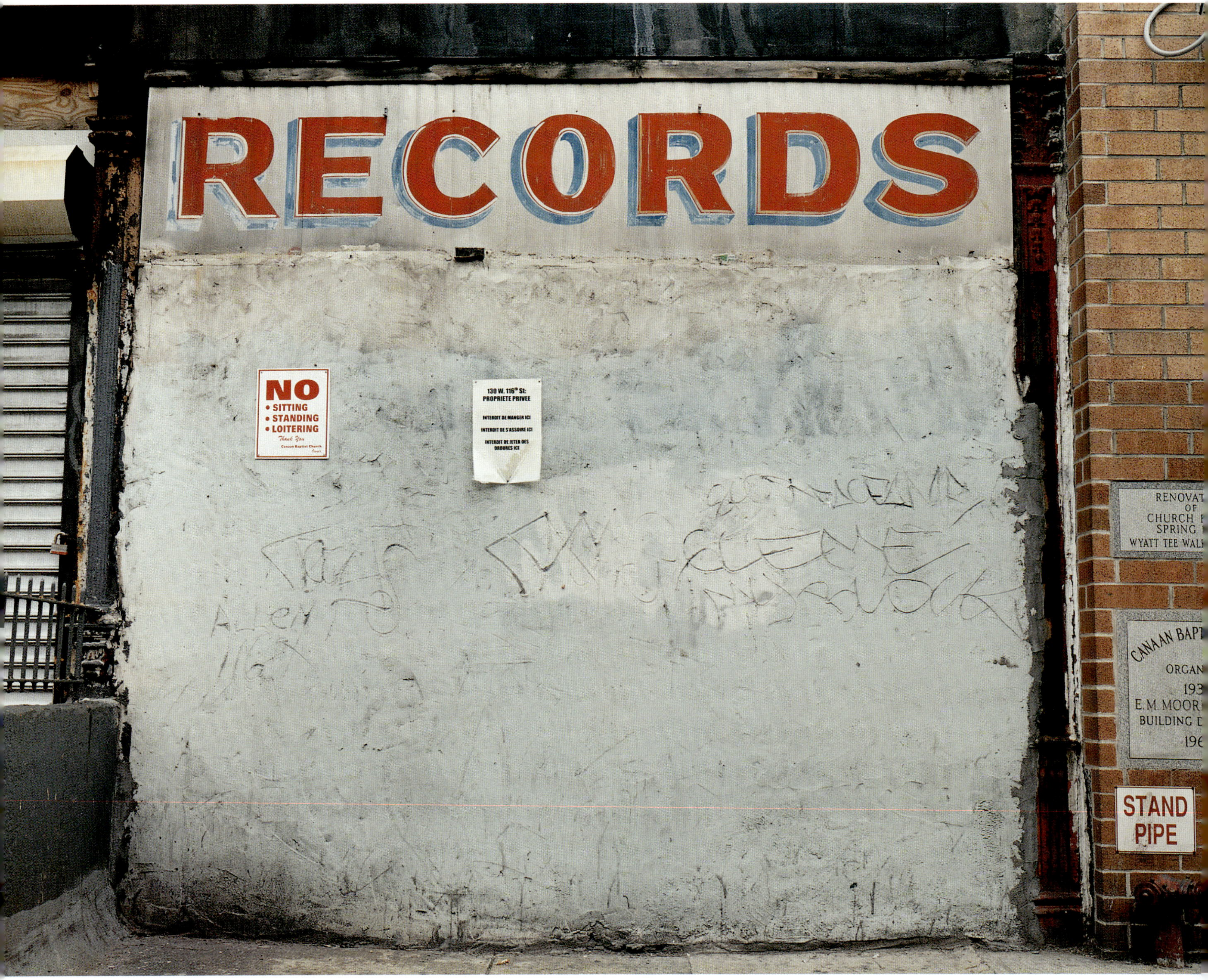
RECORDS
NO
• SITTING
• STANDING
• LOITERING
Thank You
Canaan Baptist Church
130 W. 116th St:
PROPRIETE PRIVEE
INTERDIT DE MANGER ICI
INTERDIT DE S'ASSOIRE ICI
INTERDIT DE JETER DES ORDURES ICI
STAND
PIPE

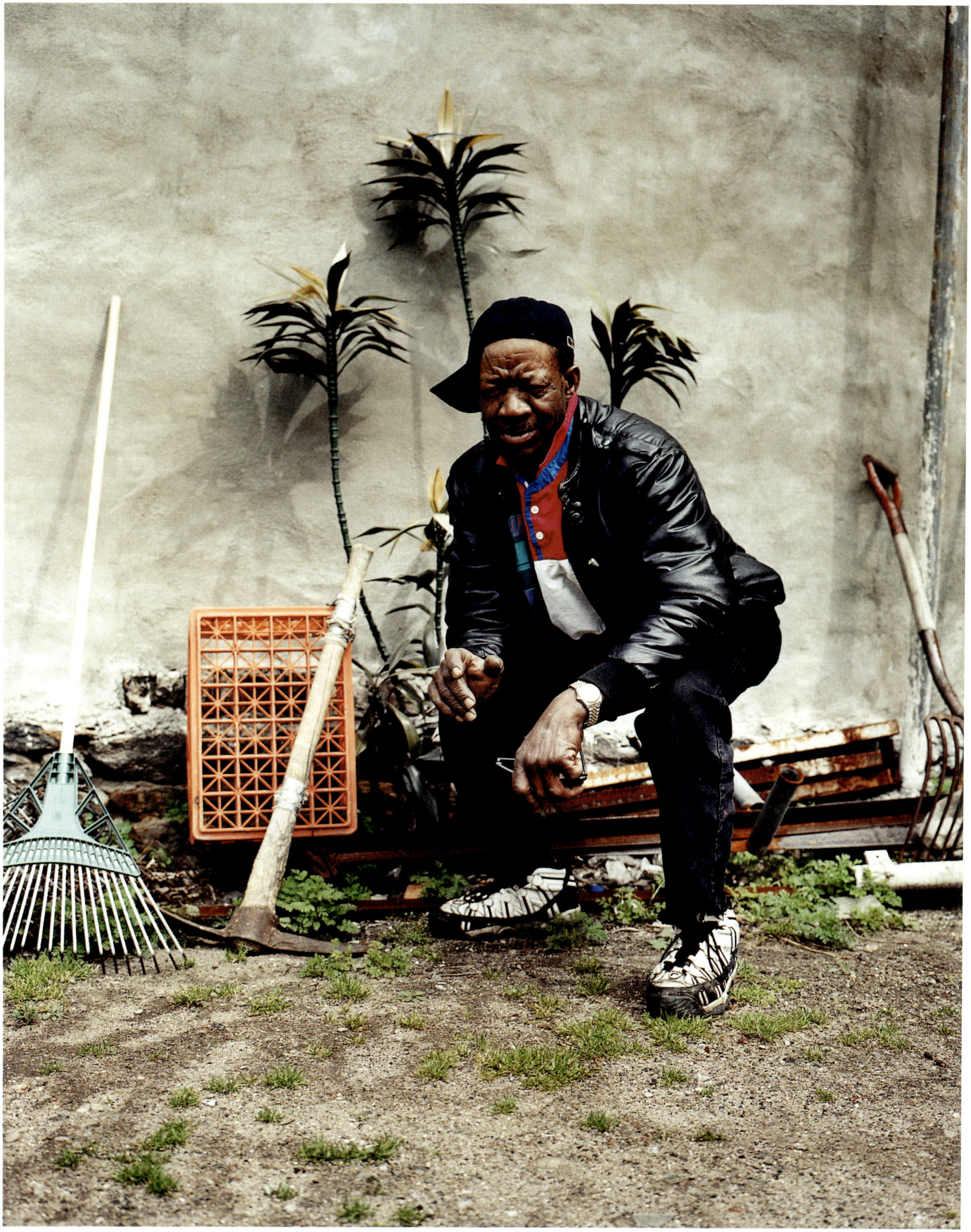

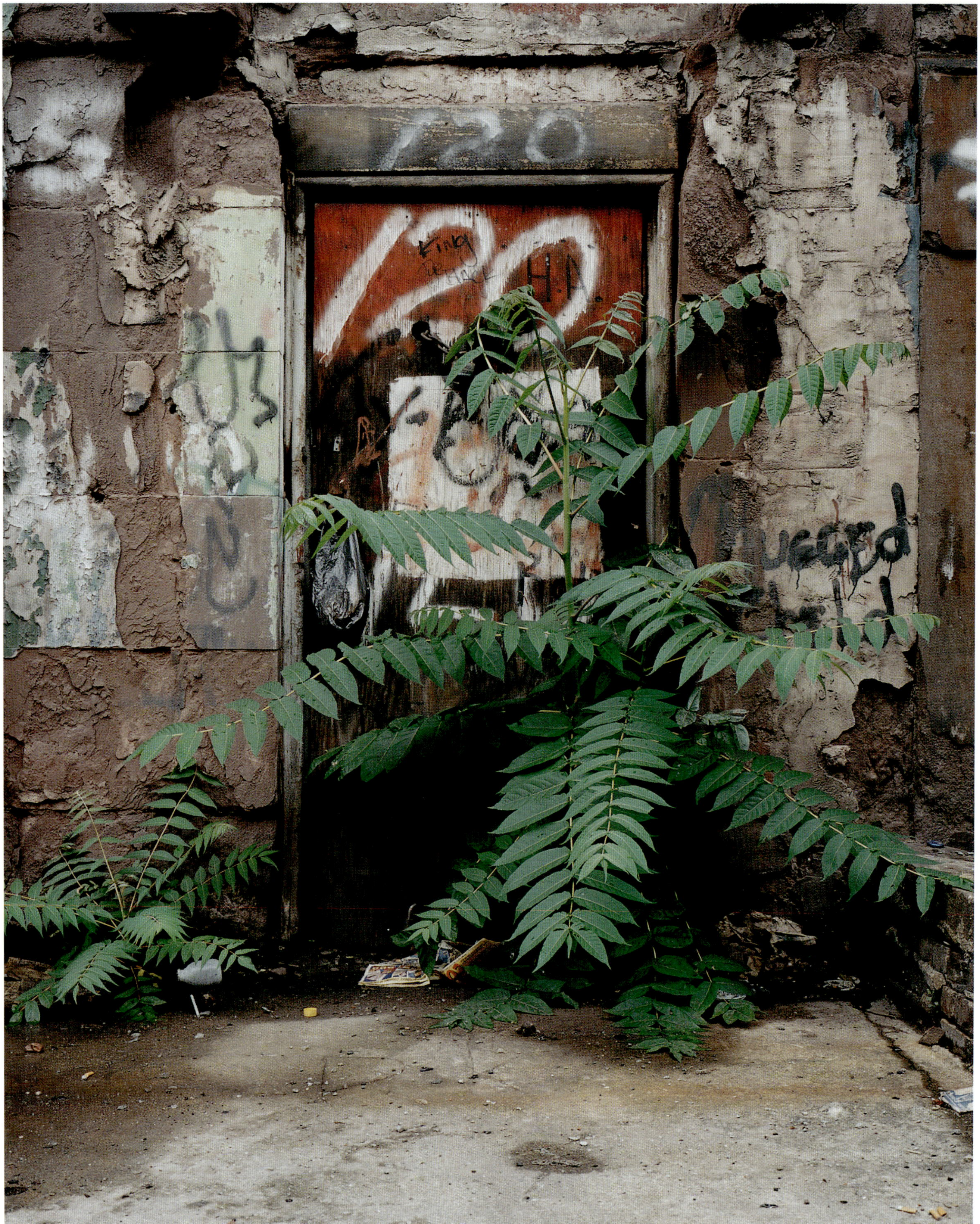
120

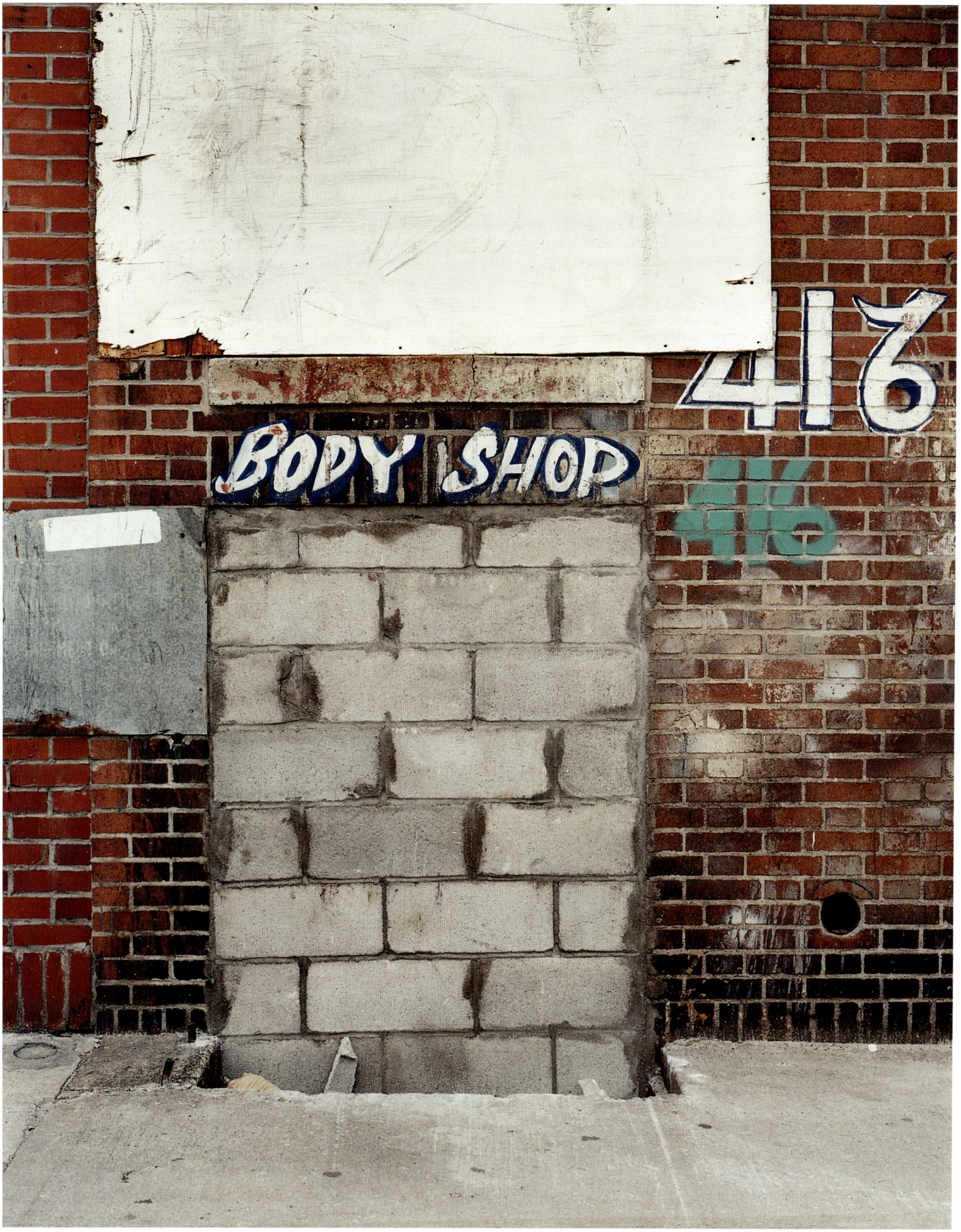
BODY SHOP
416
416

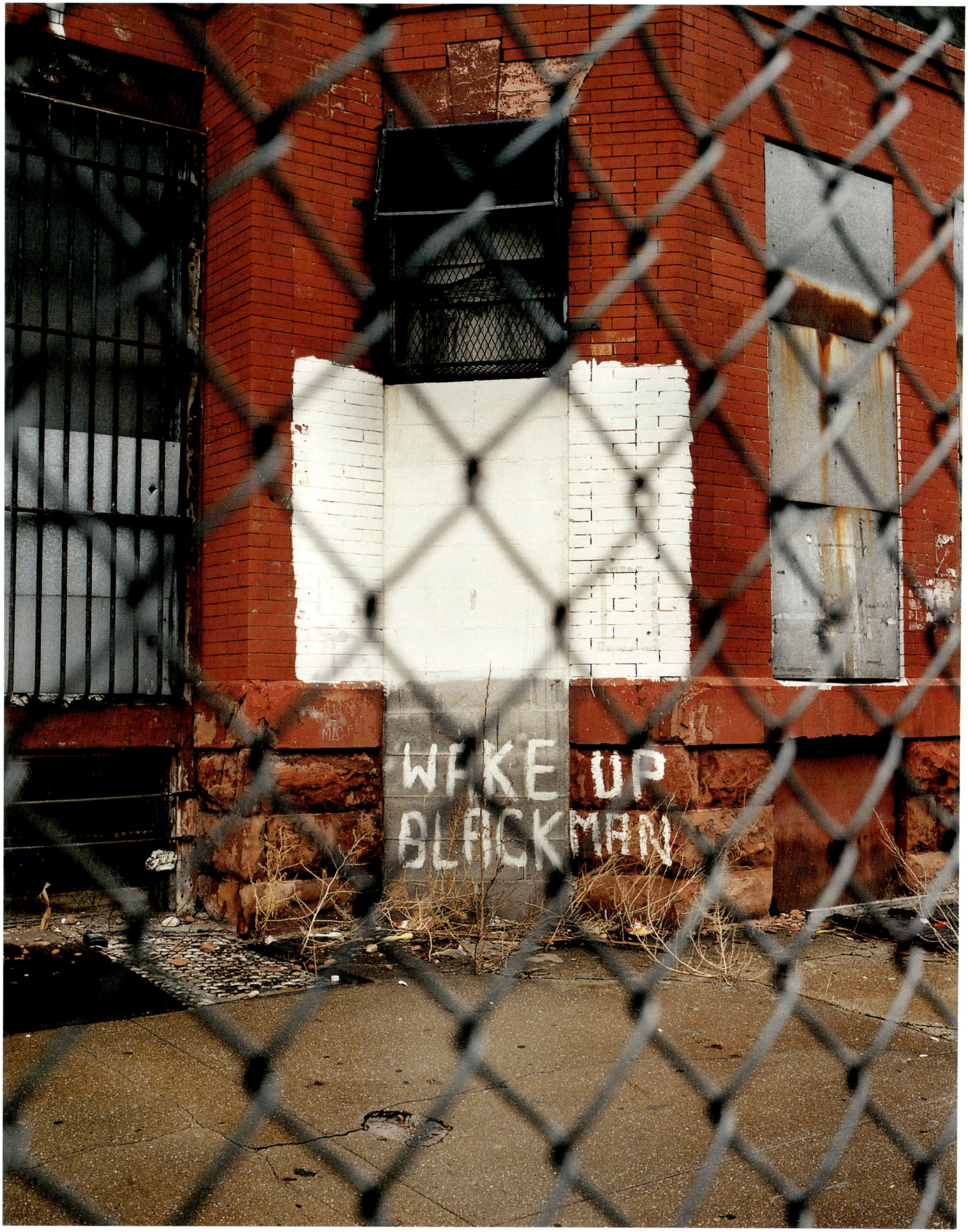
WAKE UP
BLACKMAN

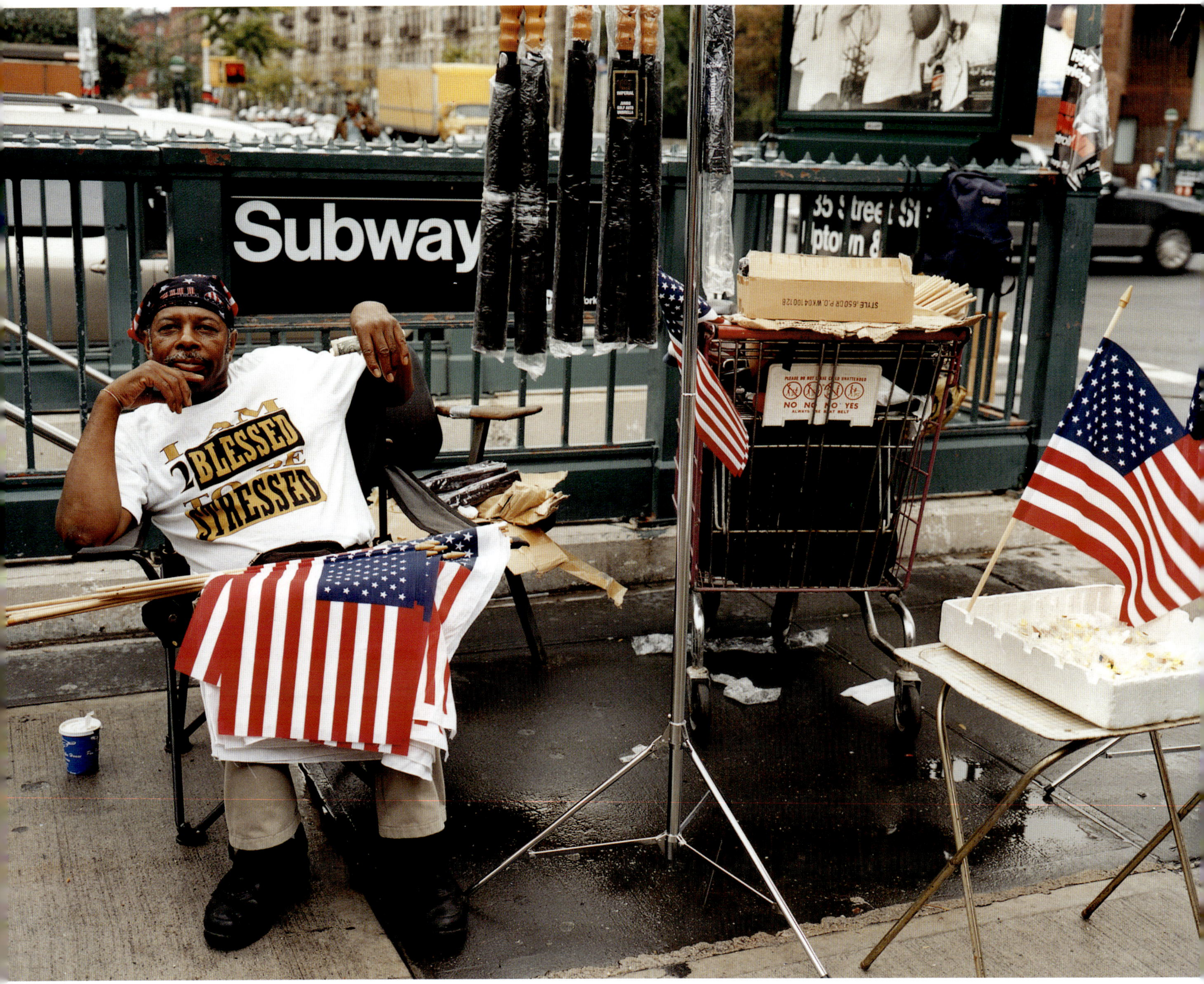
Subway
BLESSED
STRESSED

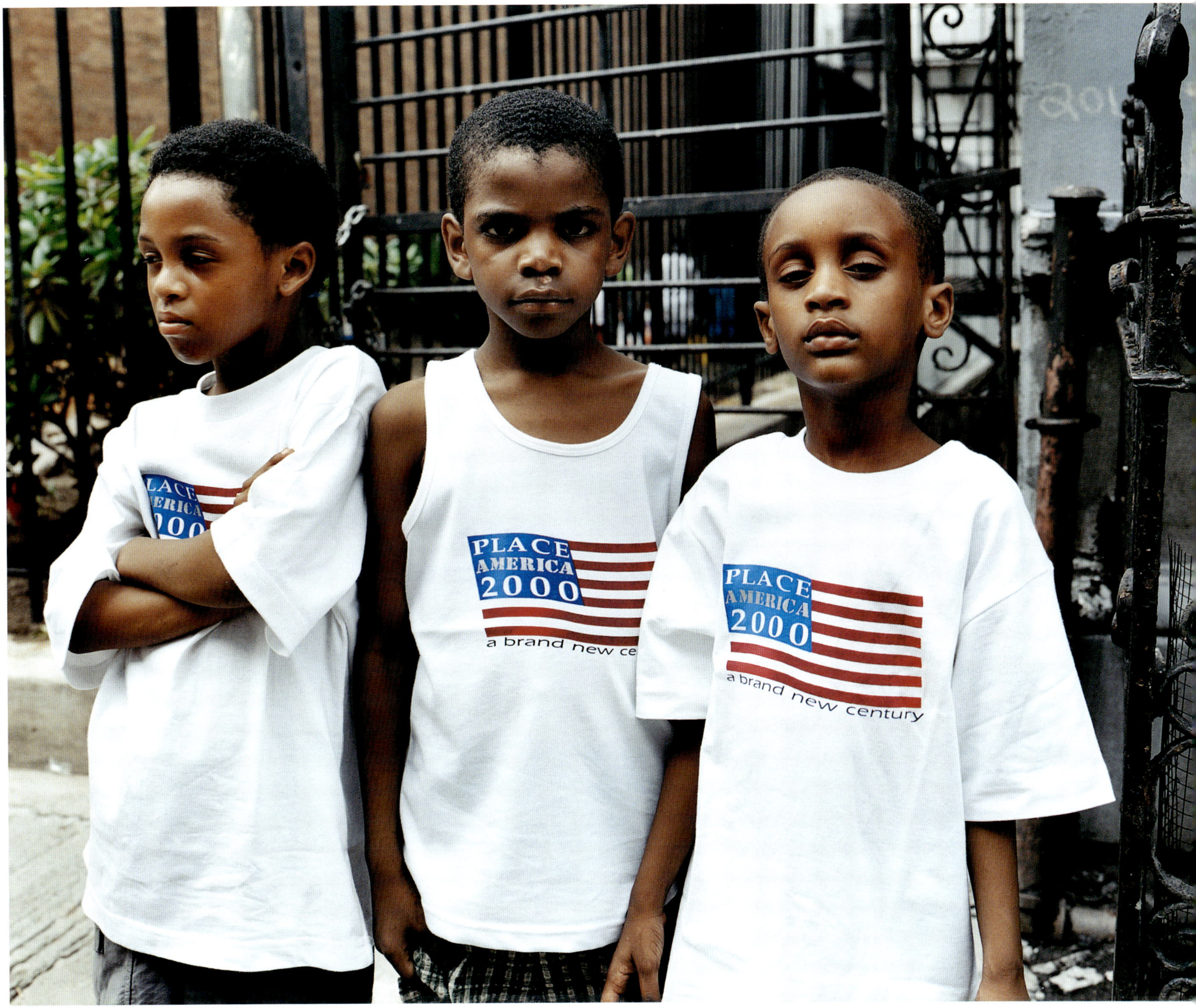
PLACE
AMERICA
2000
a brand new century

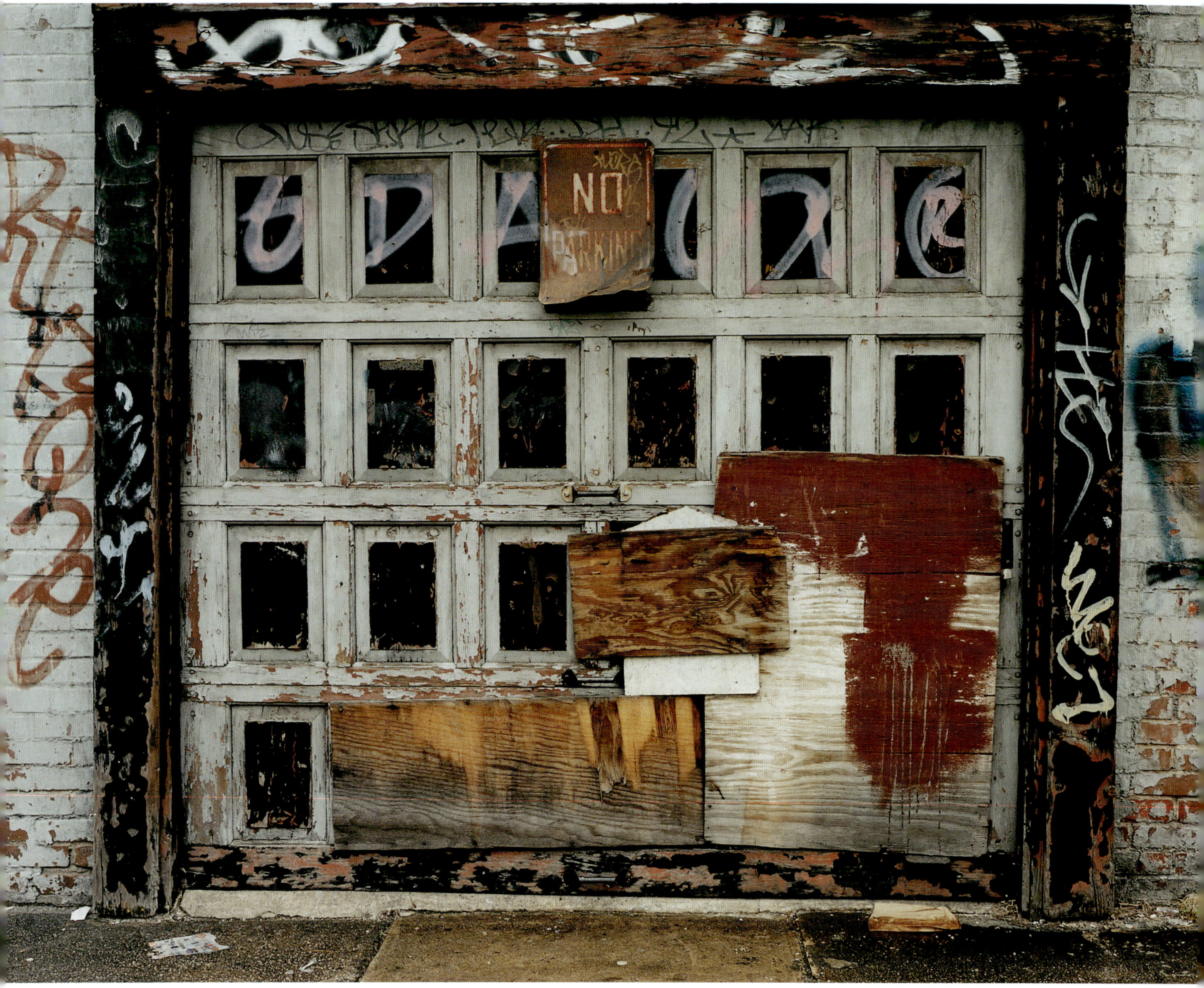
NO
PARKING

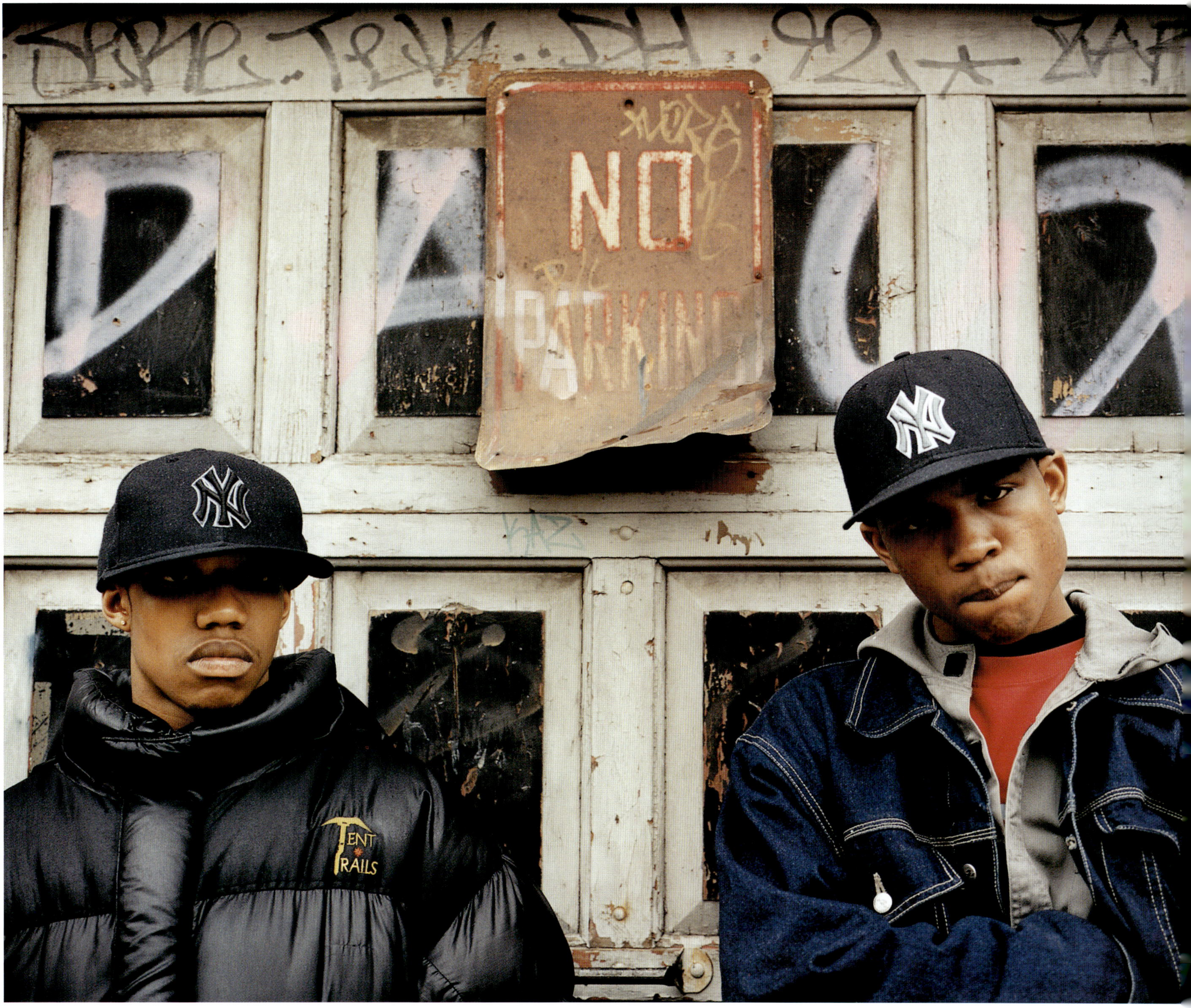
NO
PARKING
TENT
TRAILS

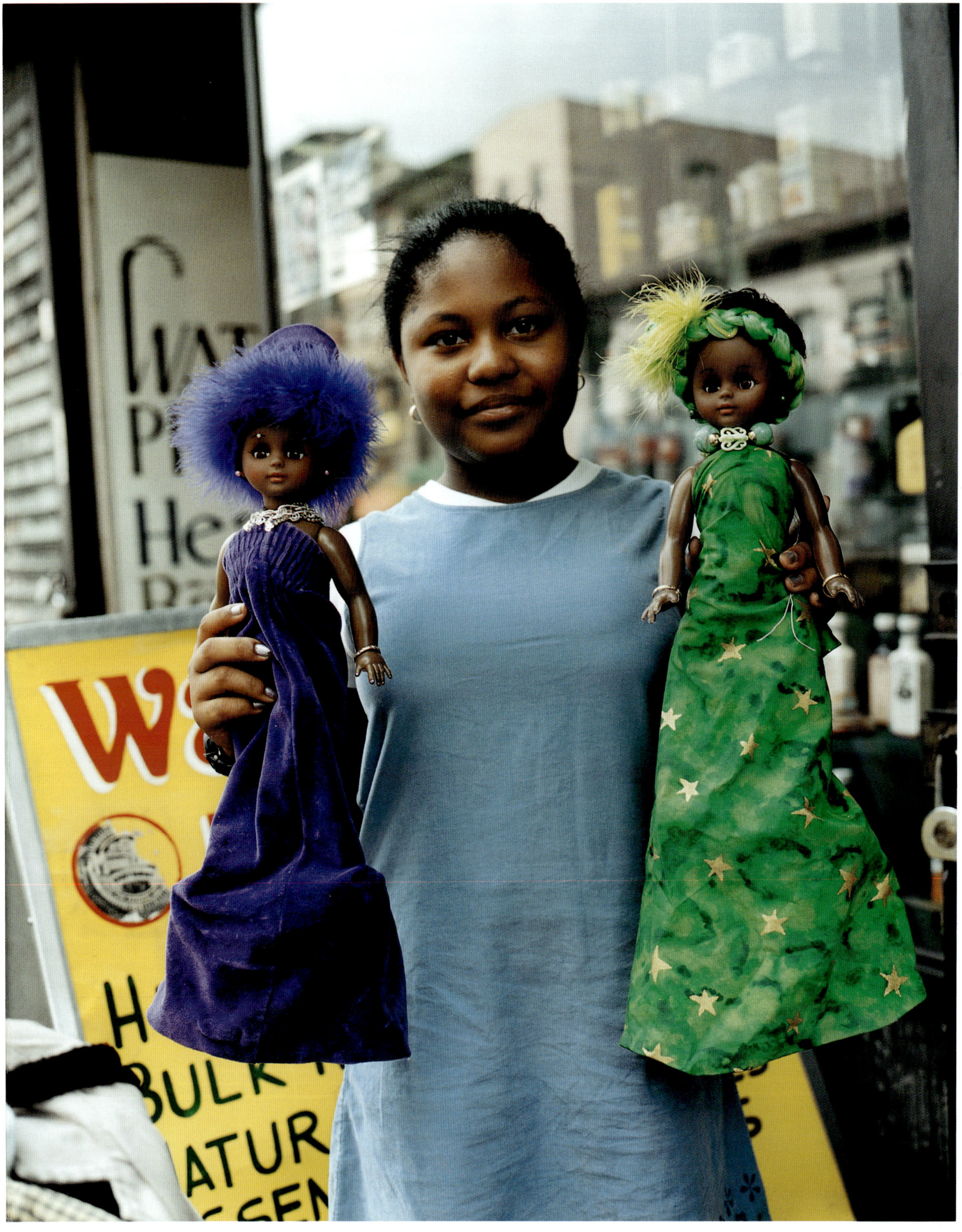

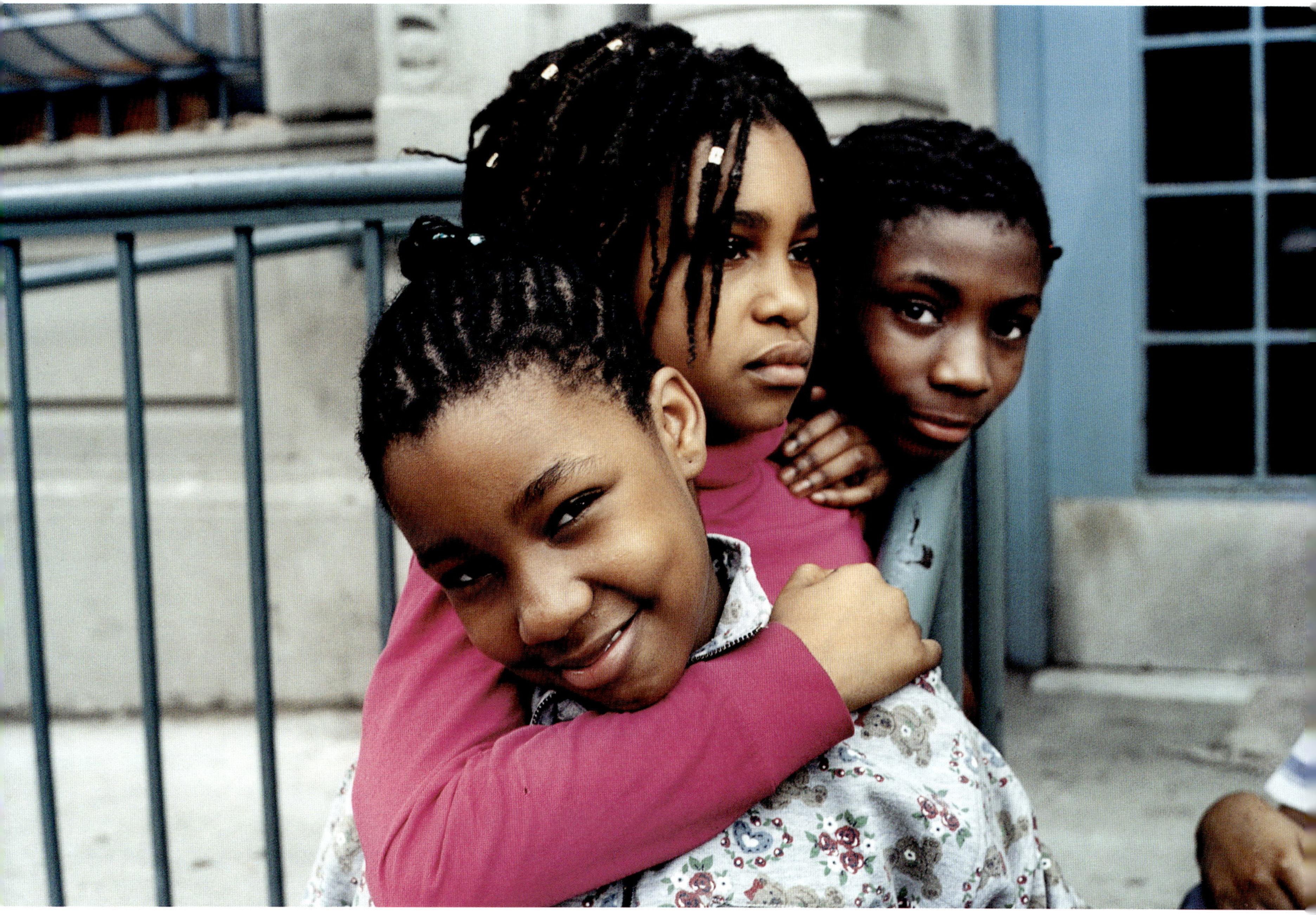

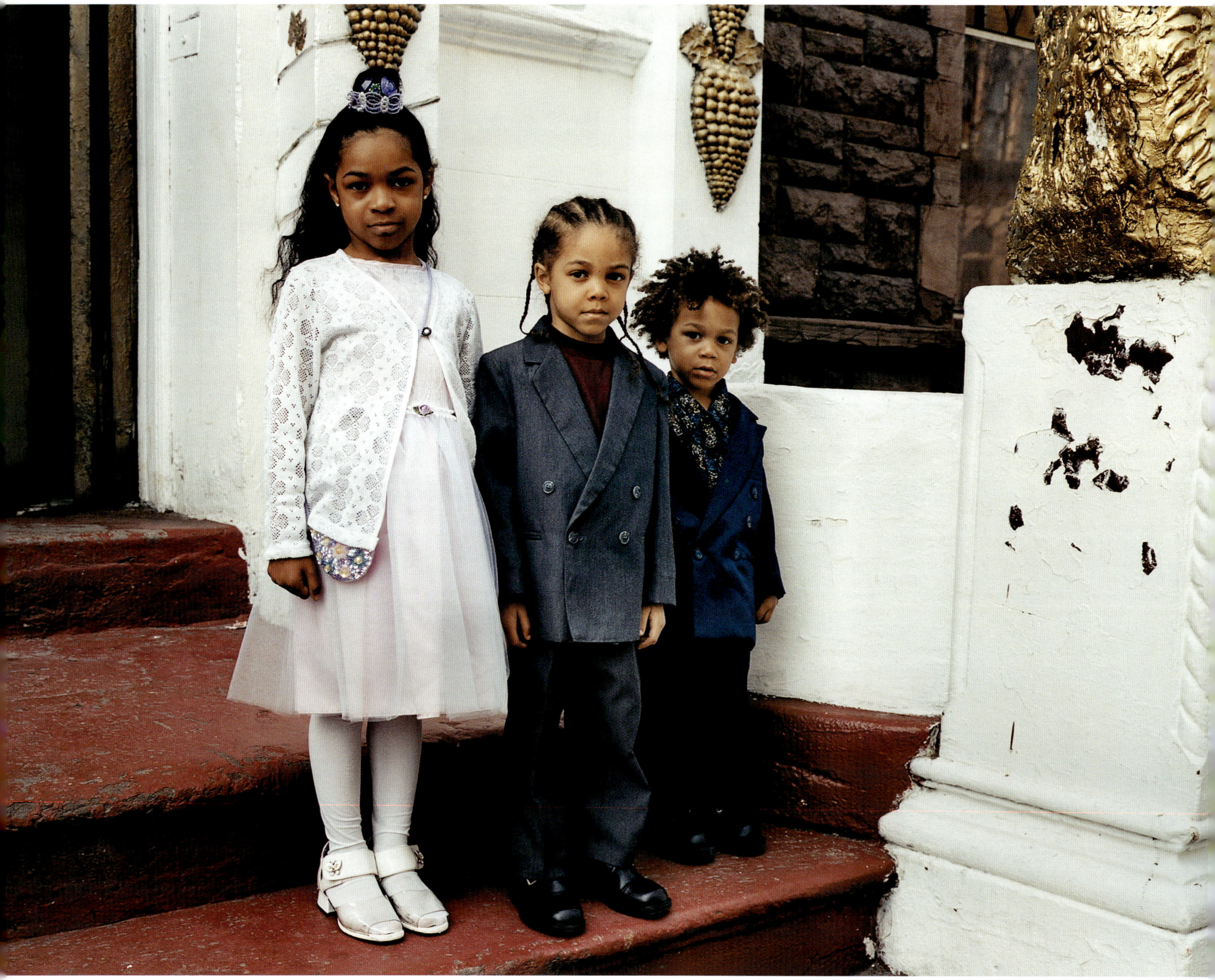

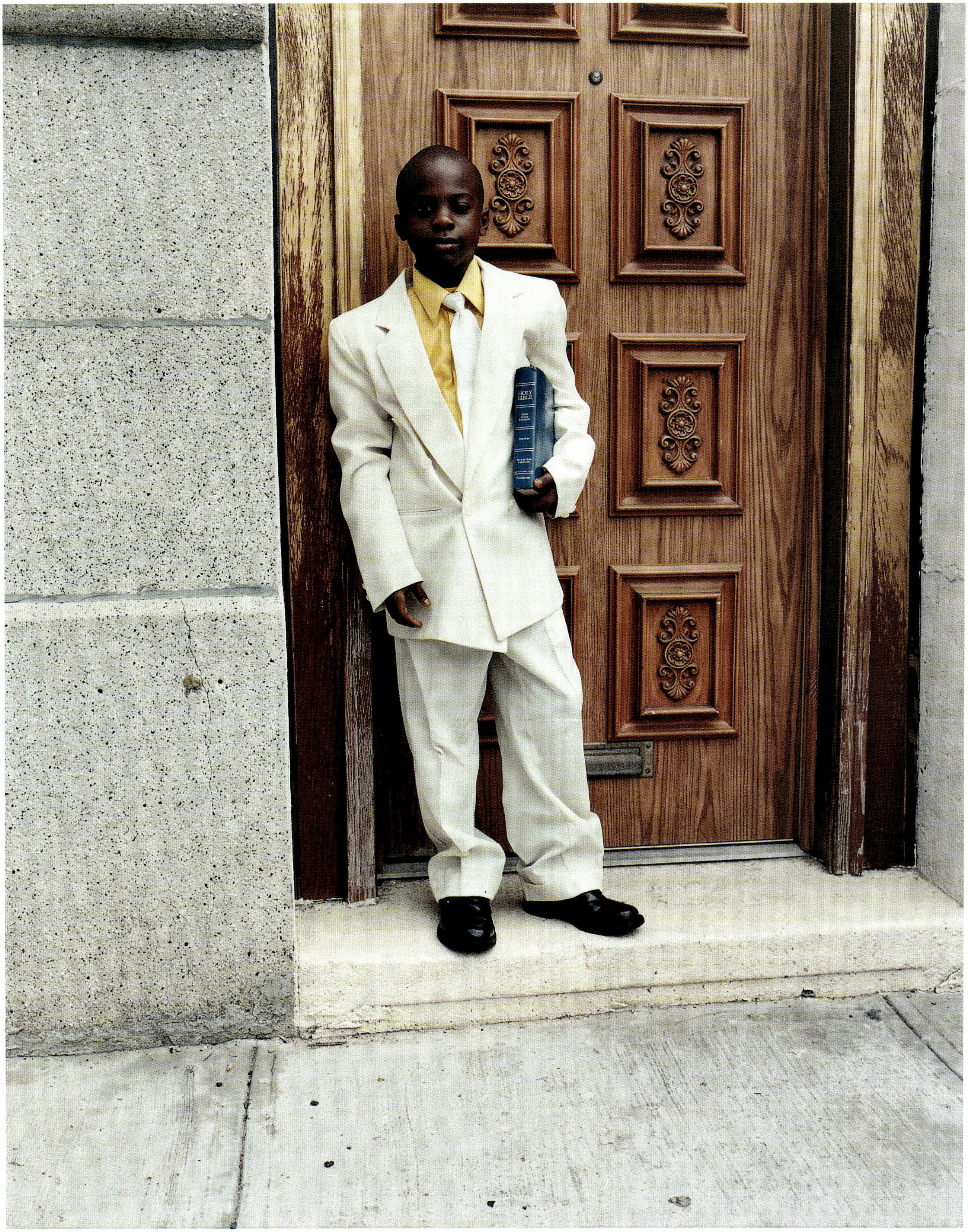
HOLY BIBLE

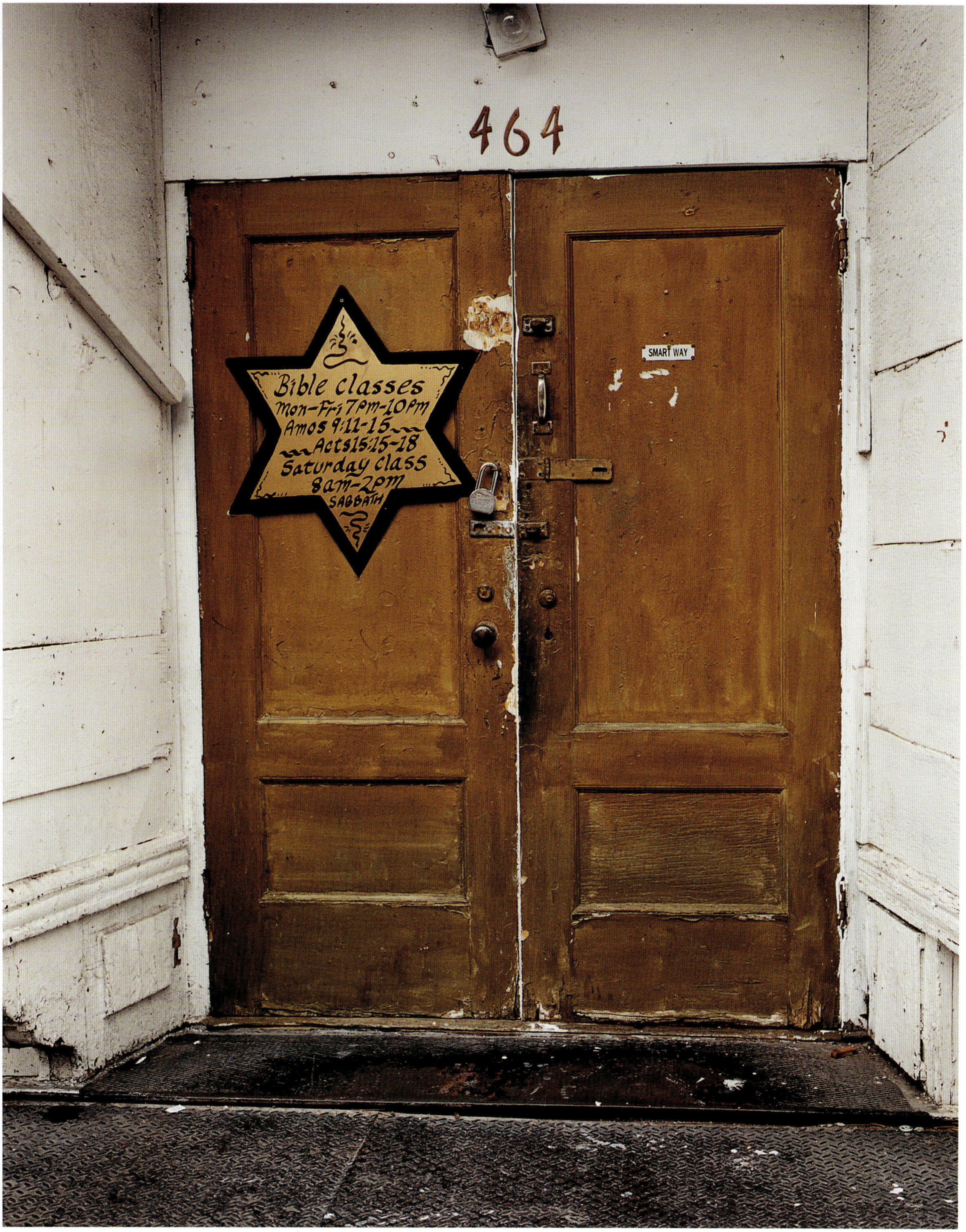
464
Bible classes
Mon-Fri 7PM-10PM
Amos 9:11-15
Acts15:15-18
Saturday class
8am-2pm
SABBATH
SMART WAY

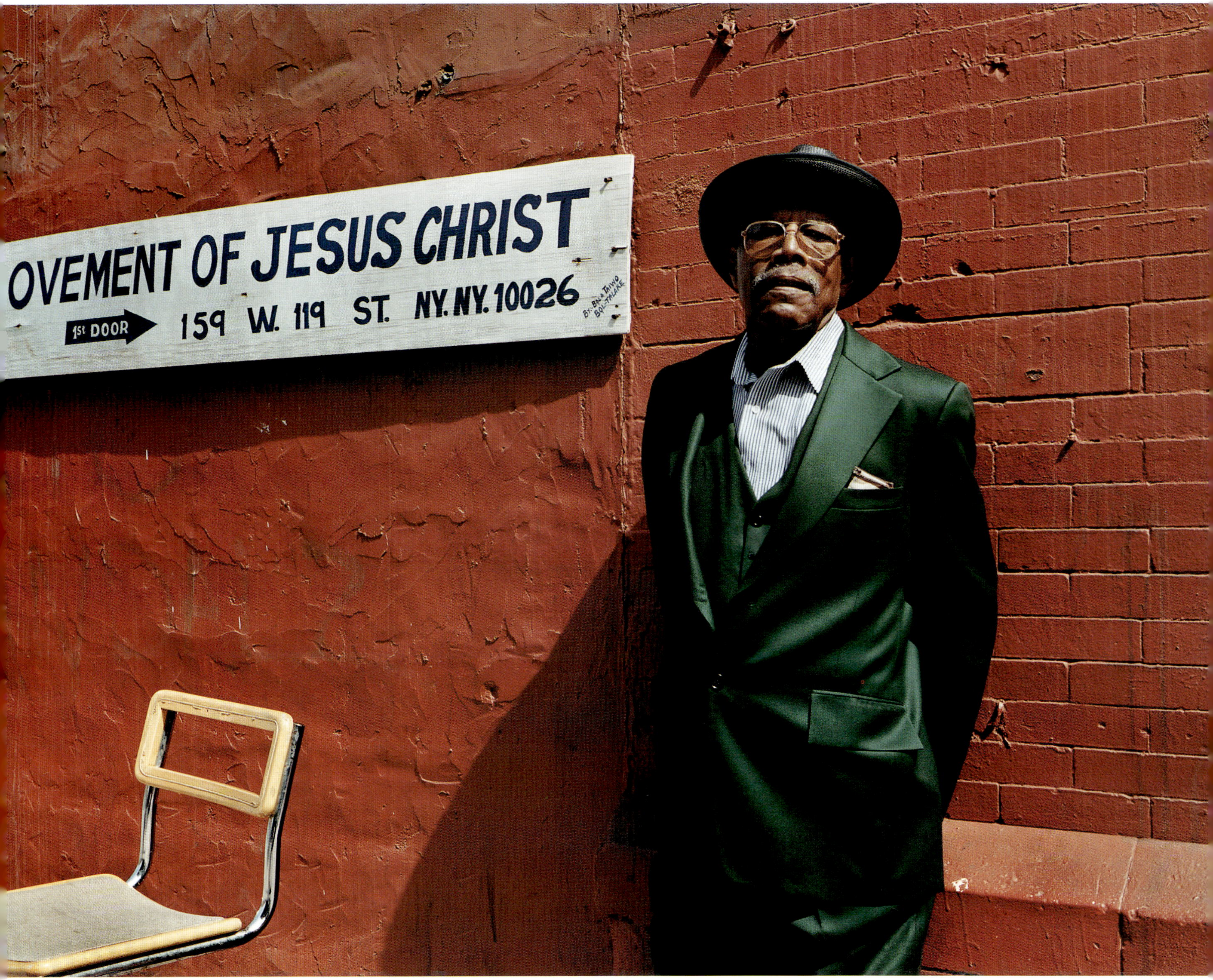
OVEMENT OF JESUS CHRIST
1st DOOR
159 W. 119 ST. NY. NY. 10026

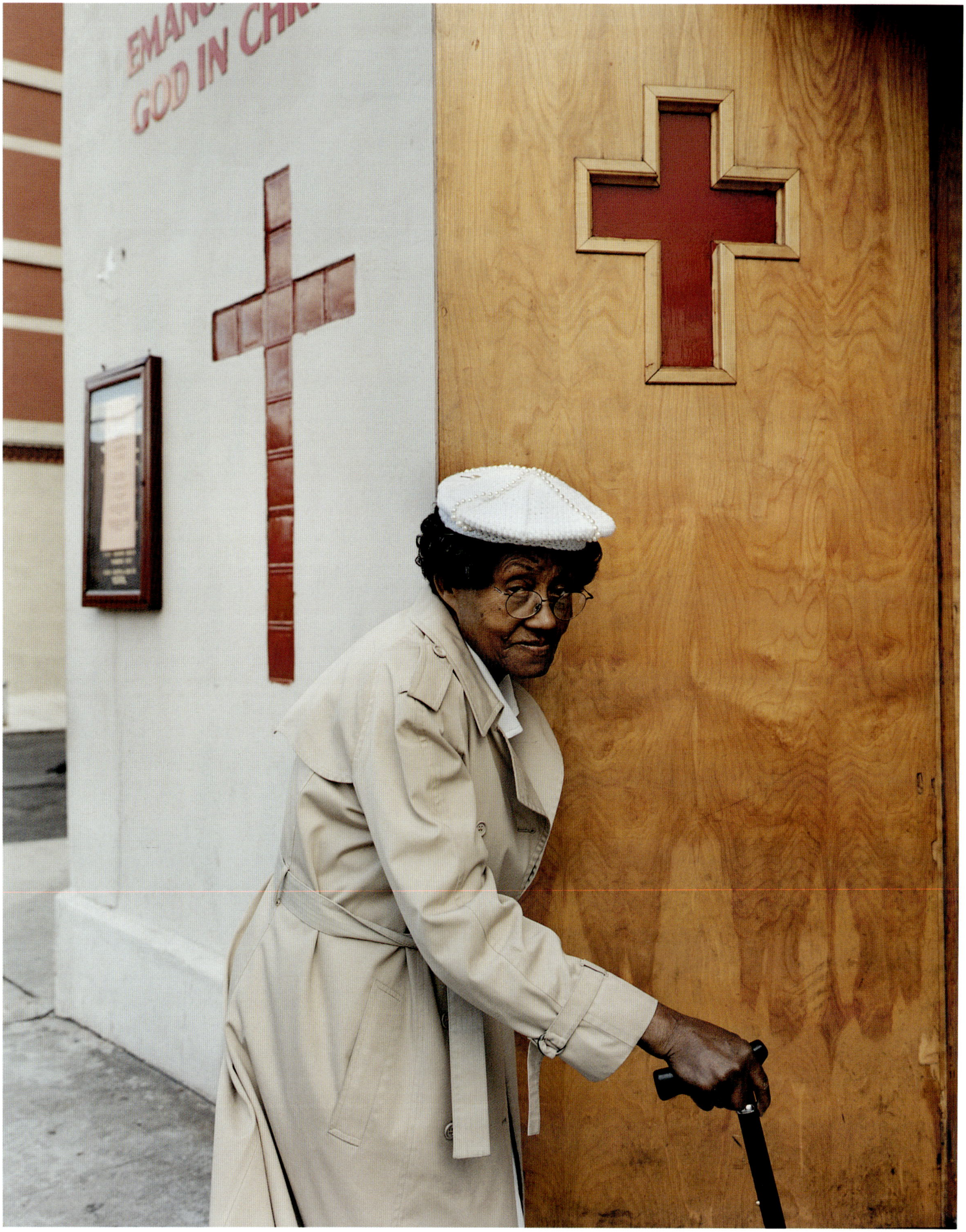

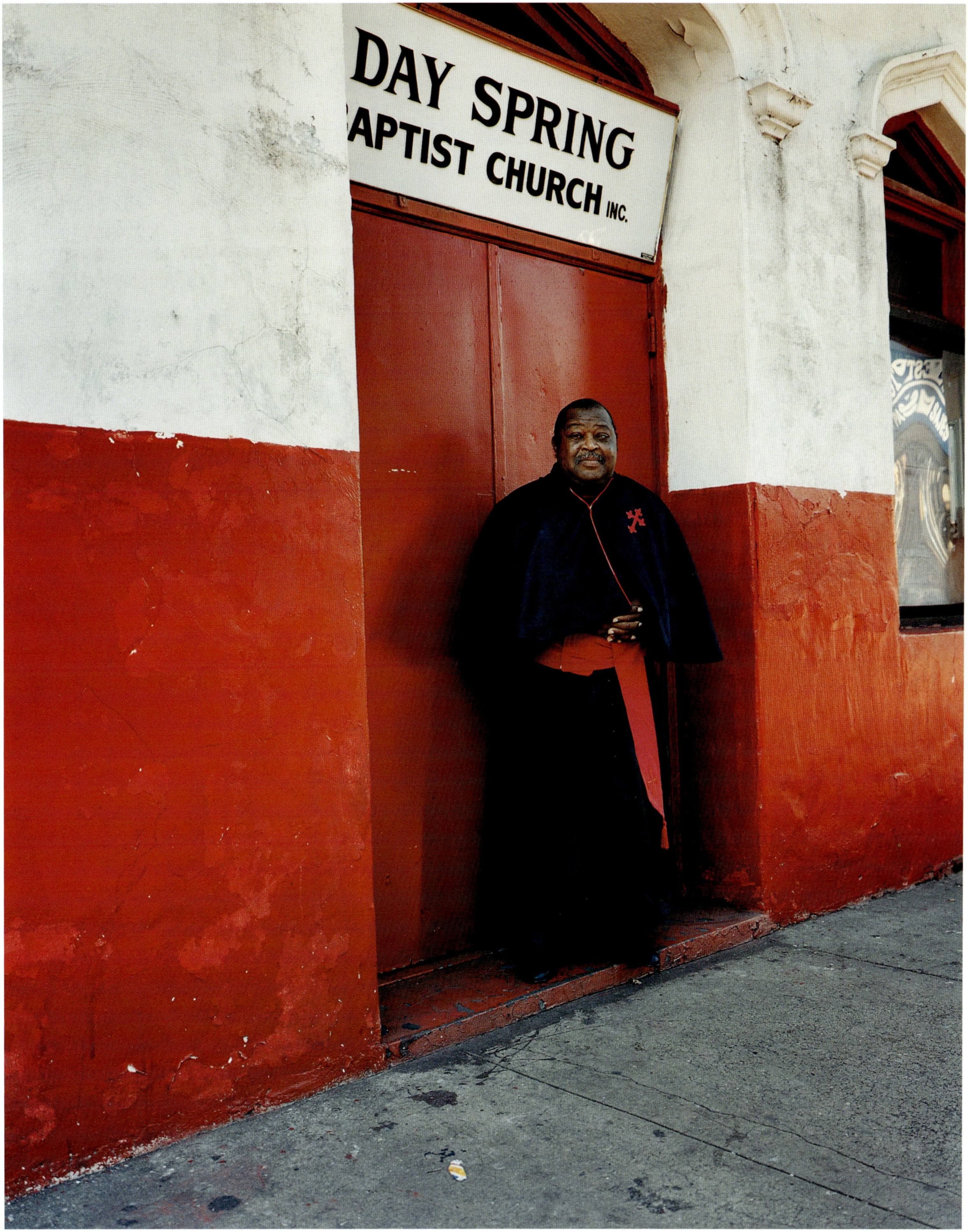
DAY SPRING
APTIST CHURCH INC.

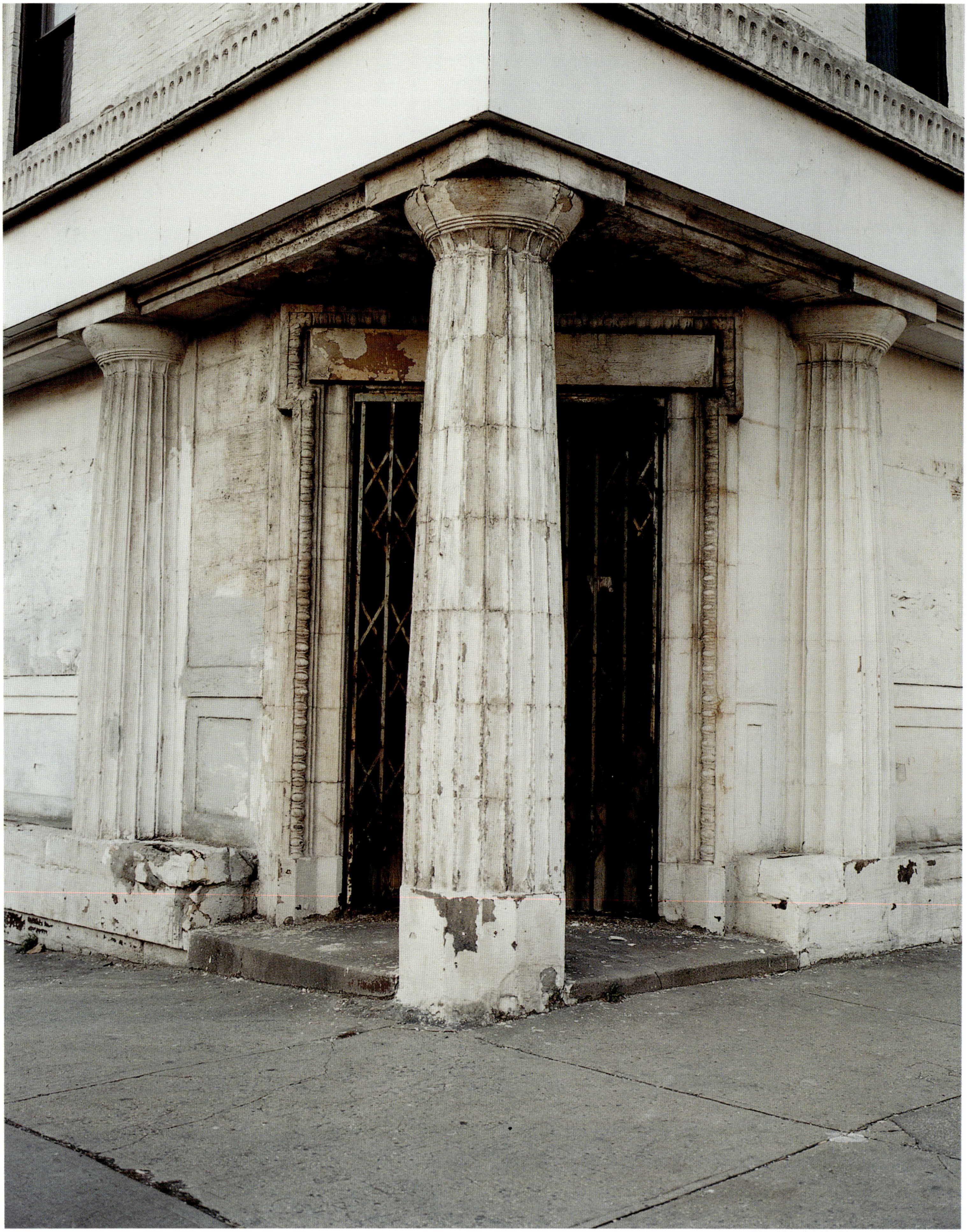

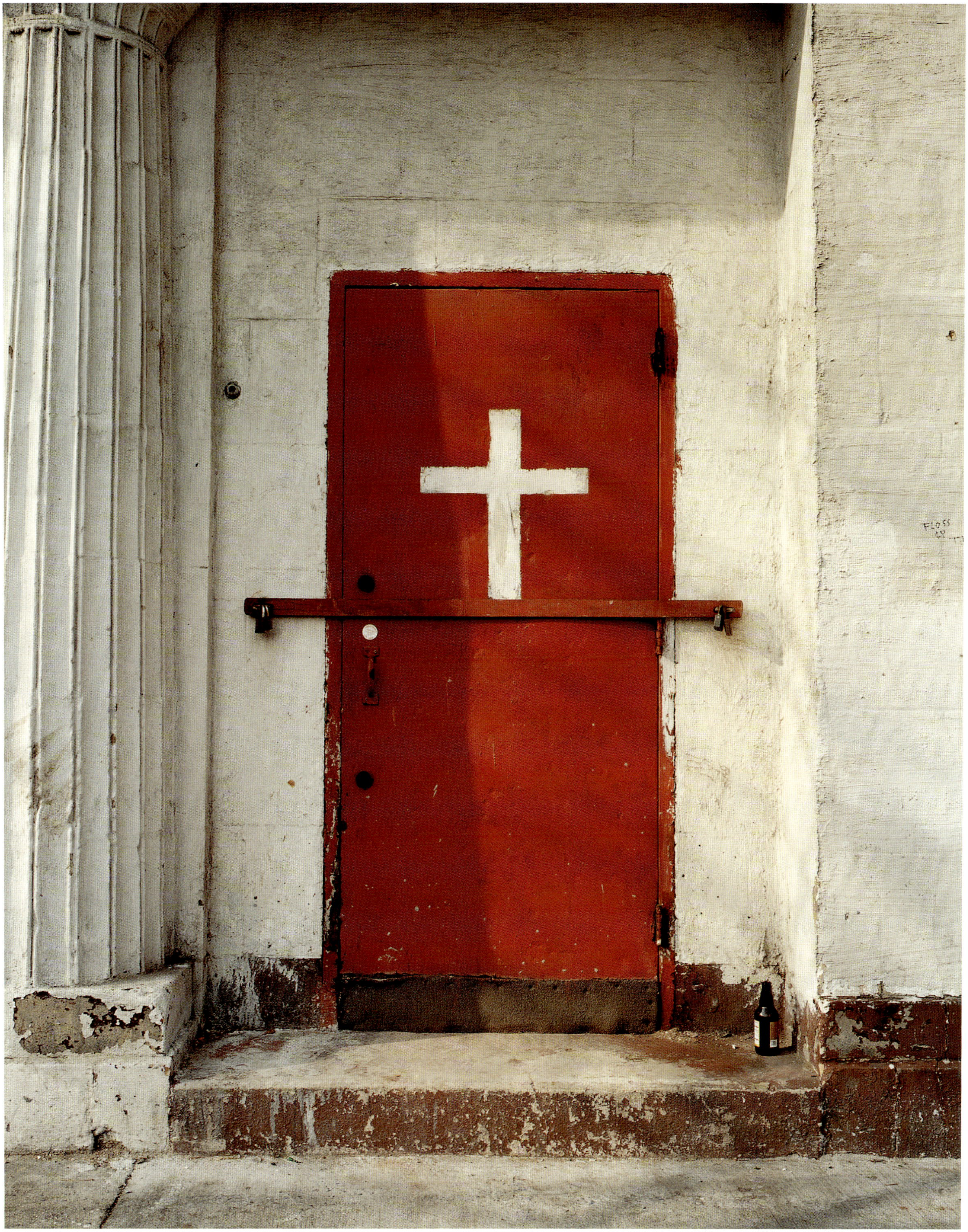

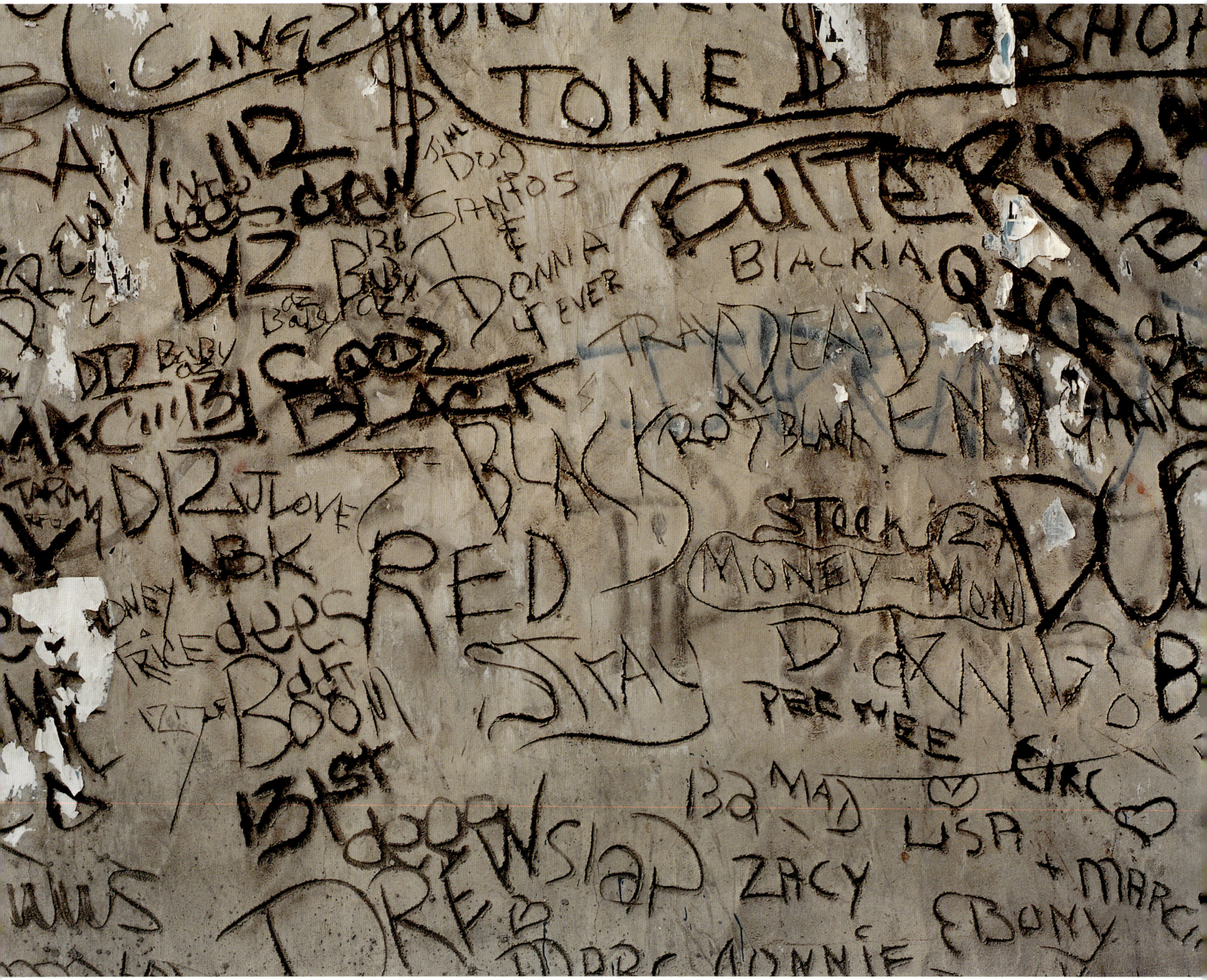
TONE
SANTOS
DONNA
4 EVER
BLACKIA
BLACK
DEAD
RED
MONEY-MON
PEE WEE
LISA
ZACY
EBONY
MAD

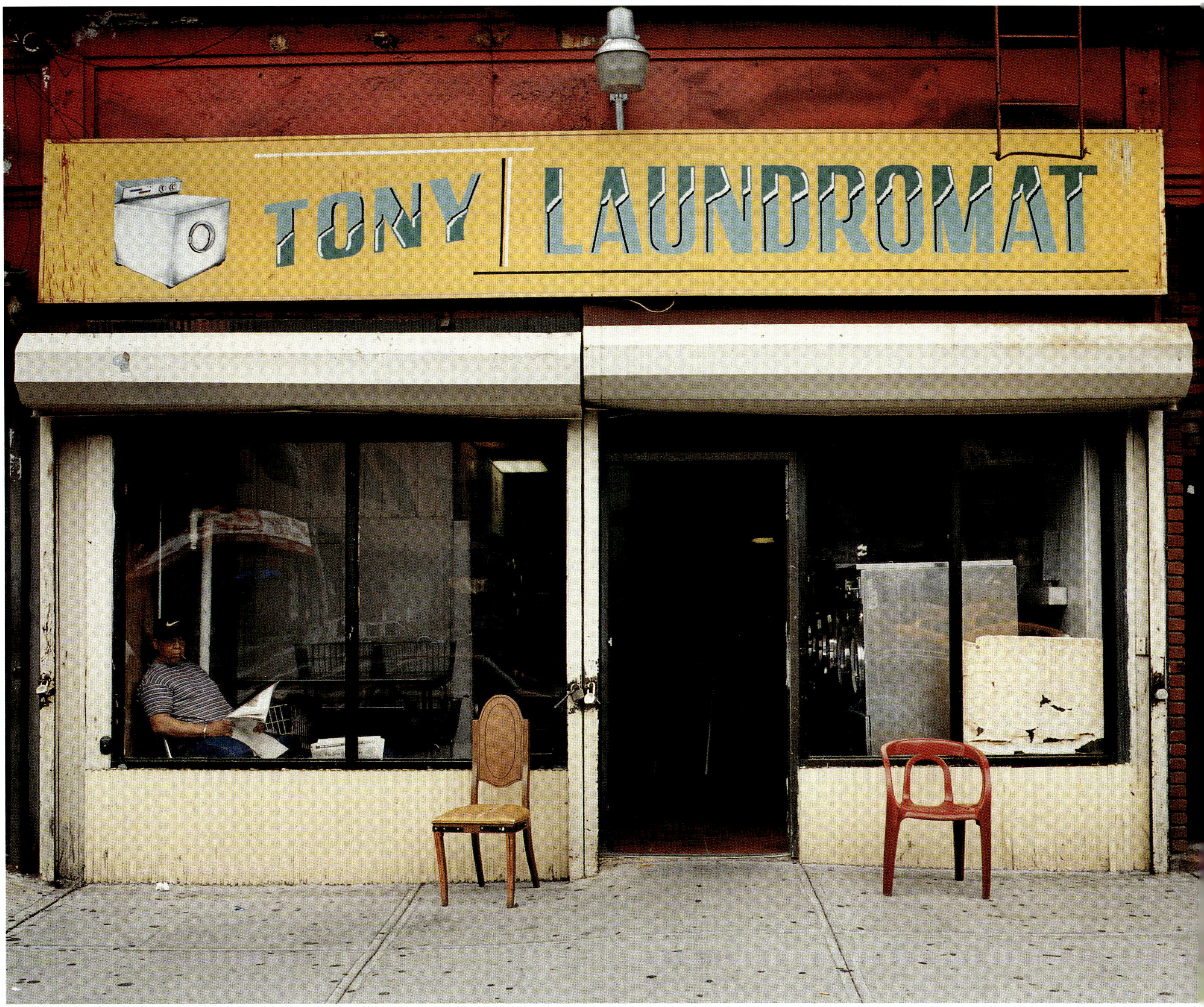
TONY
LAUNDROMAT

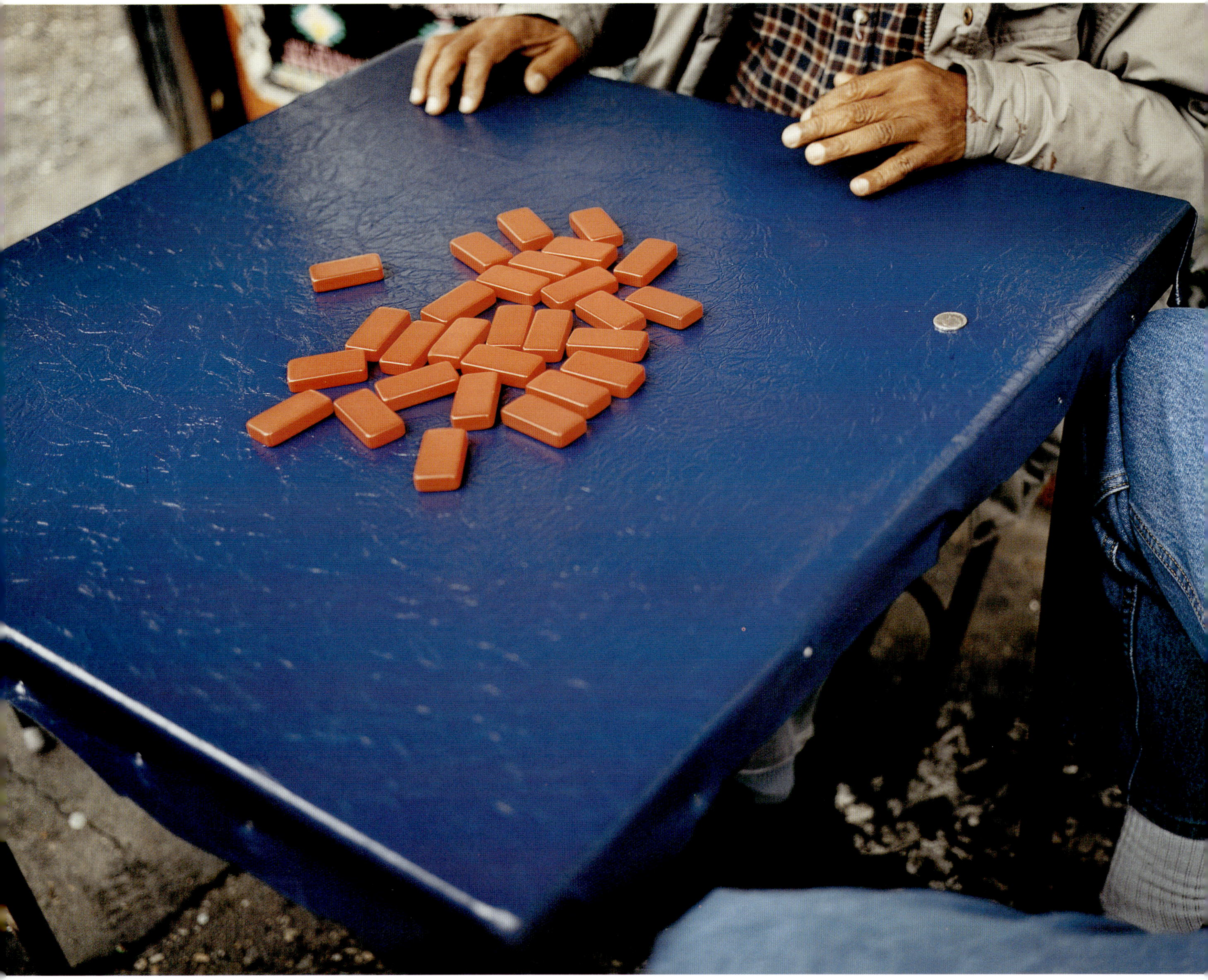

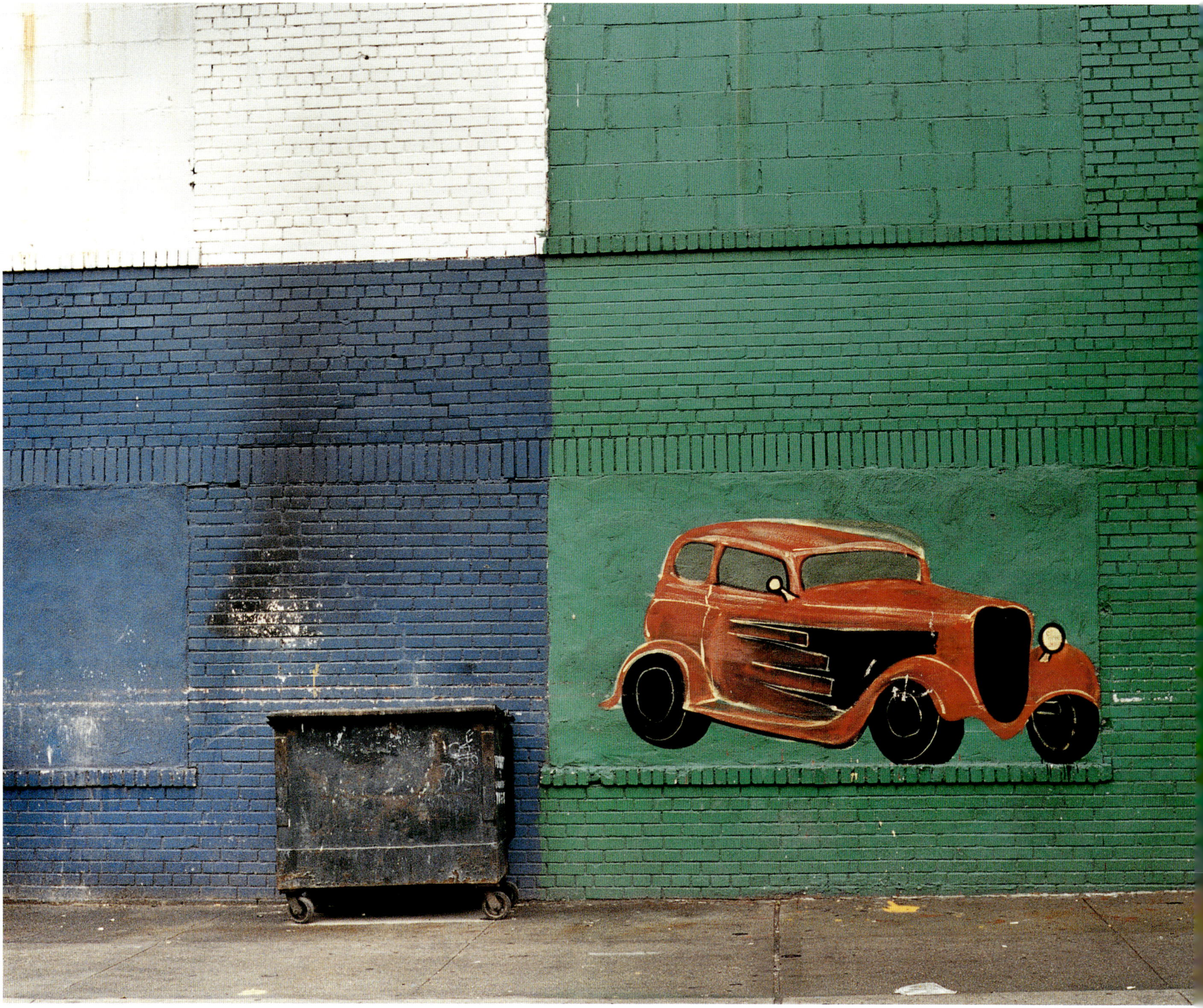

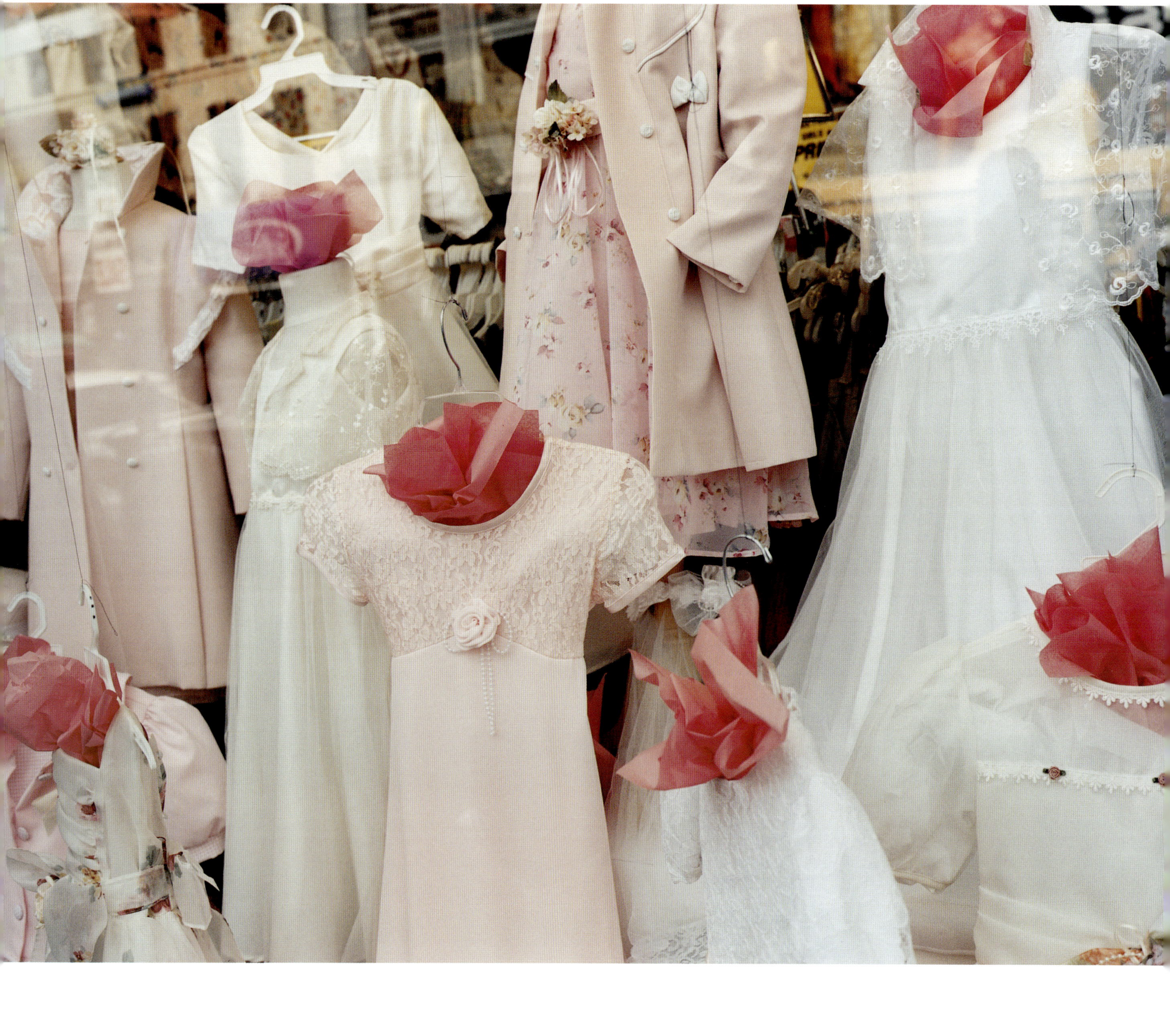

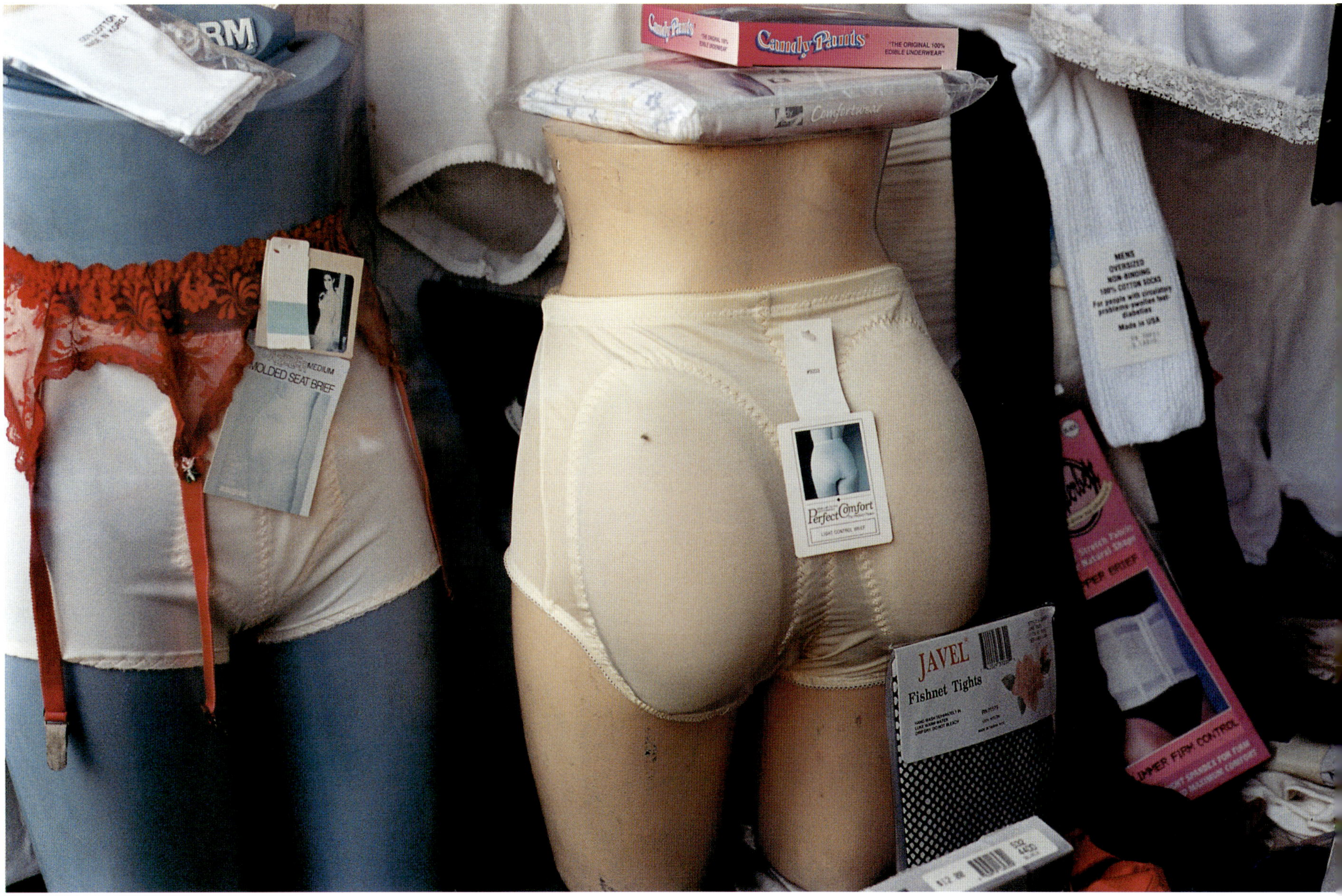

Candy Pants
"THE ORIGINAL 100% EDIBLE UNDERWEAR"
Comfortwear
MEDIUM
MOLDED SEAT BRIEF
Perfect Comfort
JAVEL
Fishnet Tights

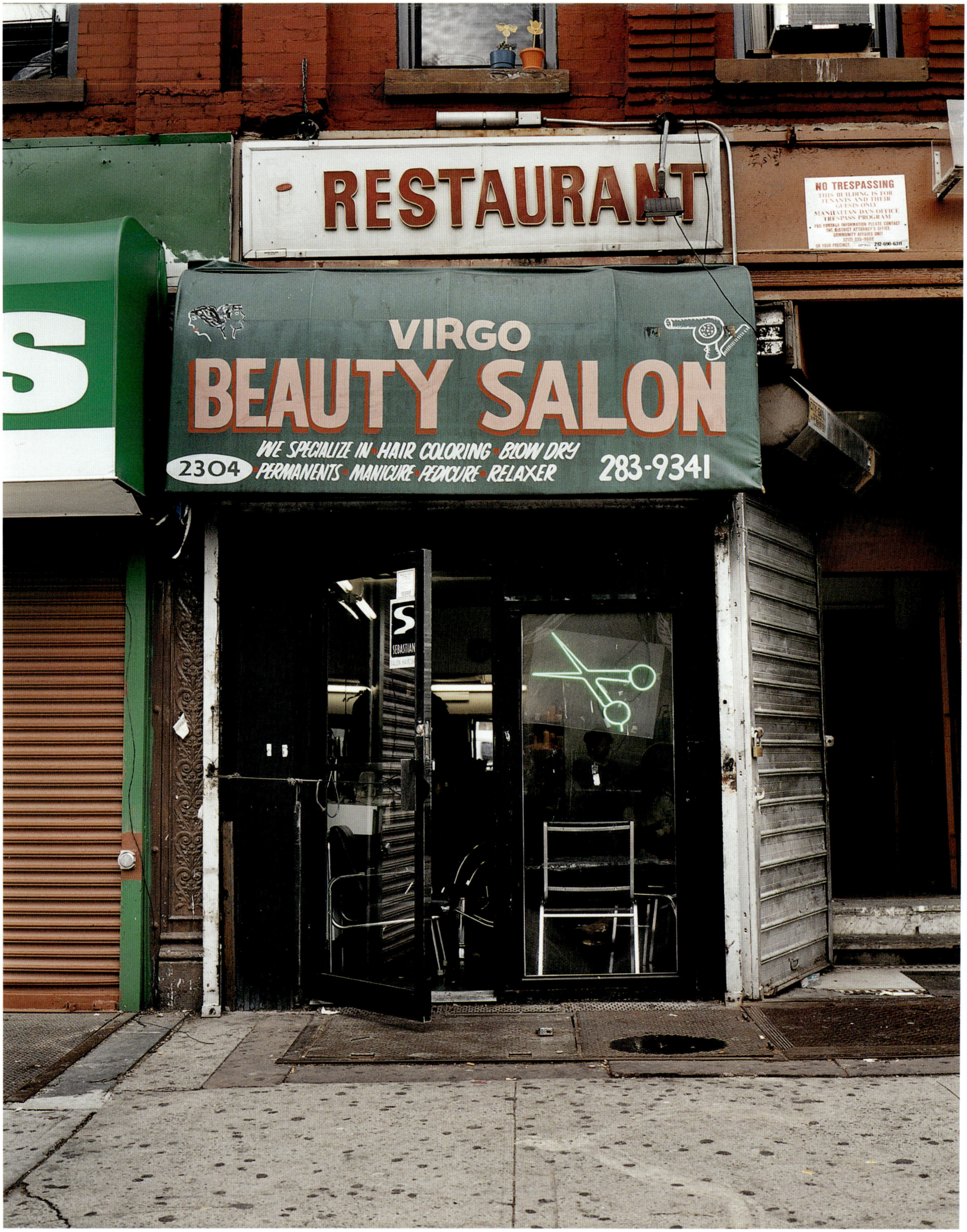
RESTAURANT
NO TRESPASSING
VIRGO
BEAUTY SALON
WE SPECIALIZE IN • HAIR COLORING • BLOW DRY
2304
• PERMANENTS • MANICURE • PEDICURE • RELAXER
283-9341
SEBASTIAN

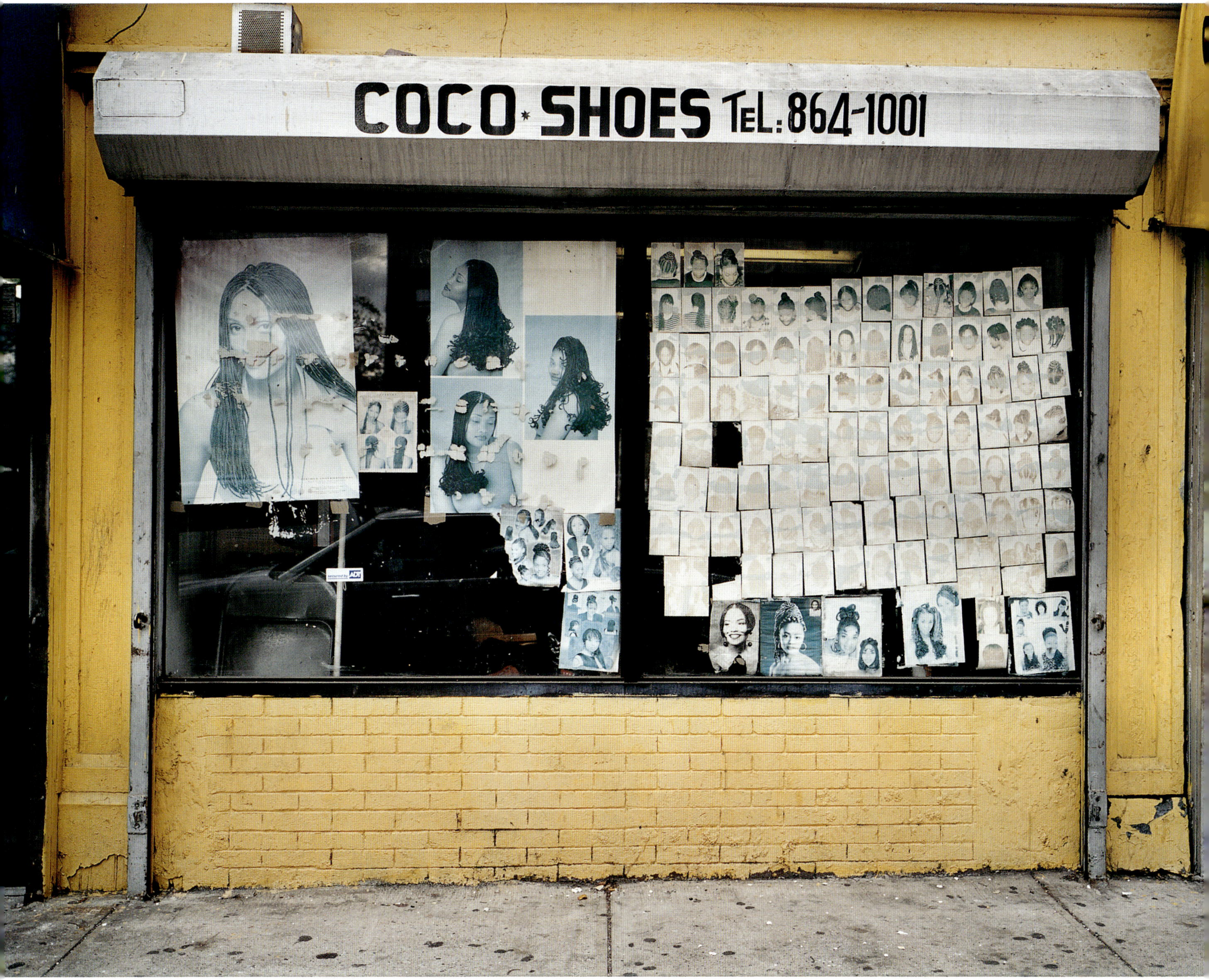
COCO SHOES TEL: 864-1001

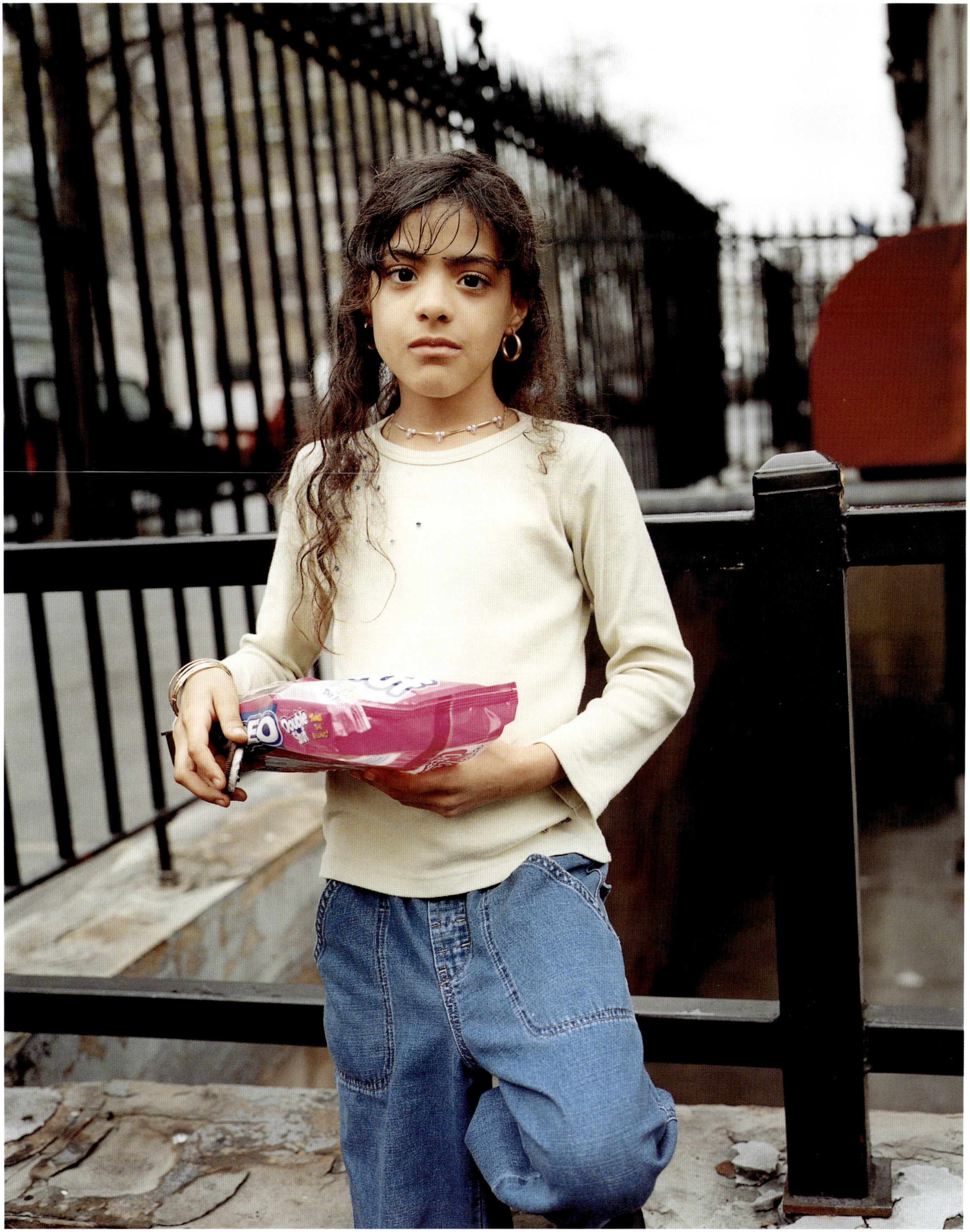

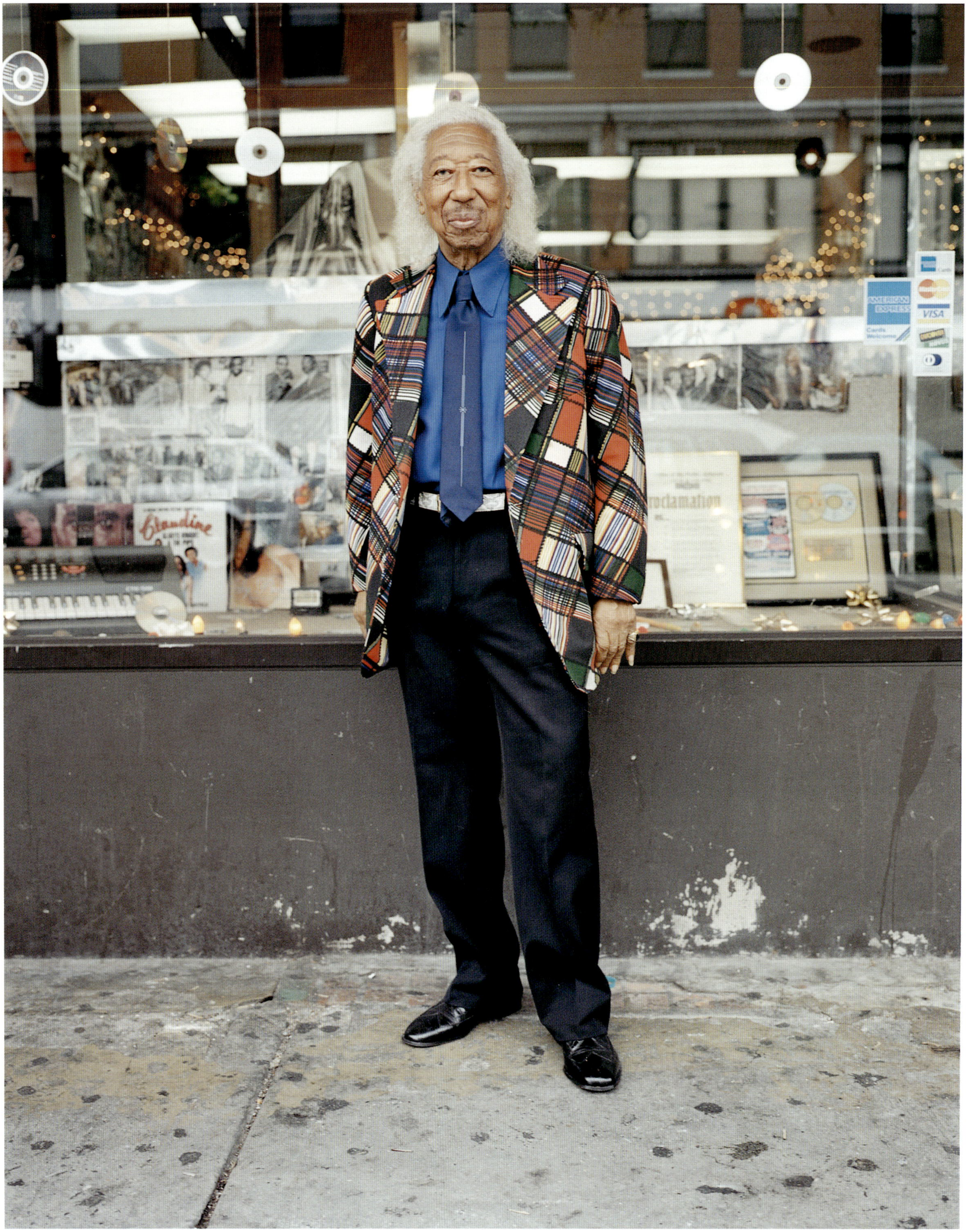
AMERICAN EXPRESS
VISA

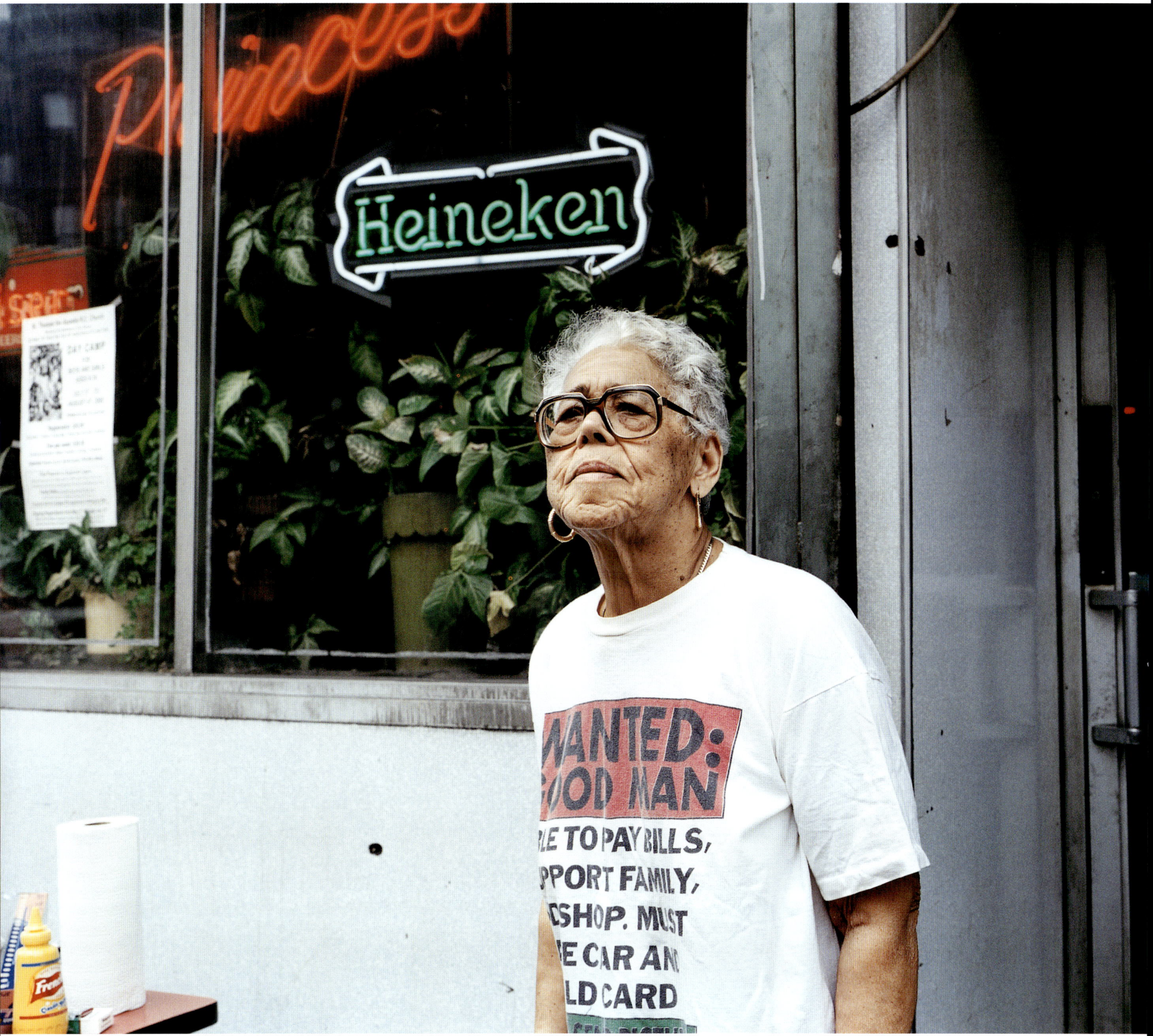
Heineken
ANTED:
OOD MAN
LE TO PAY BILLS,
PPORT FAMILY,
CSHOP. MUST
E CAR AN
LD CARD

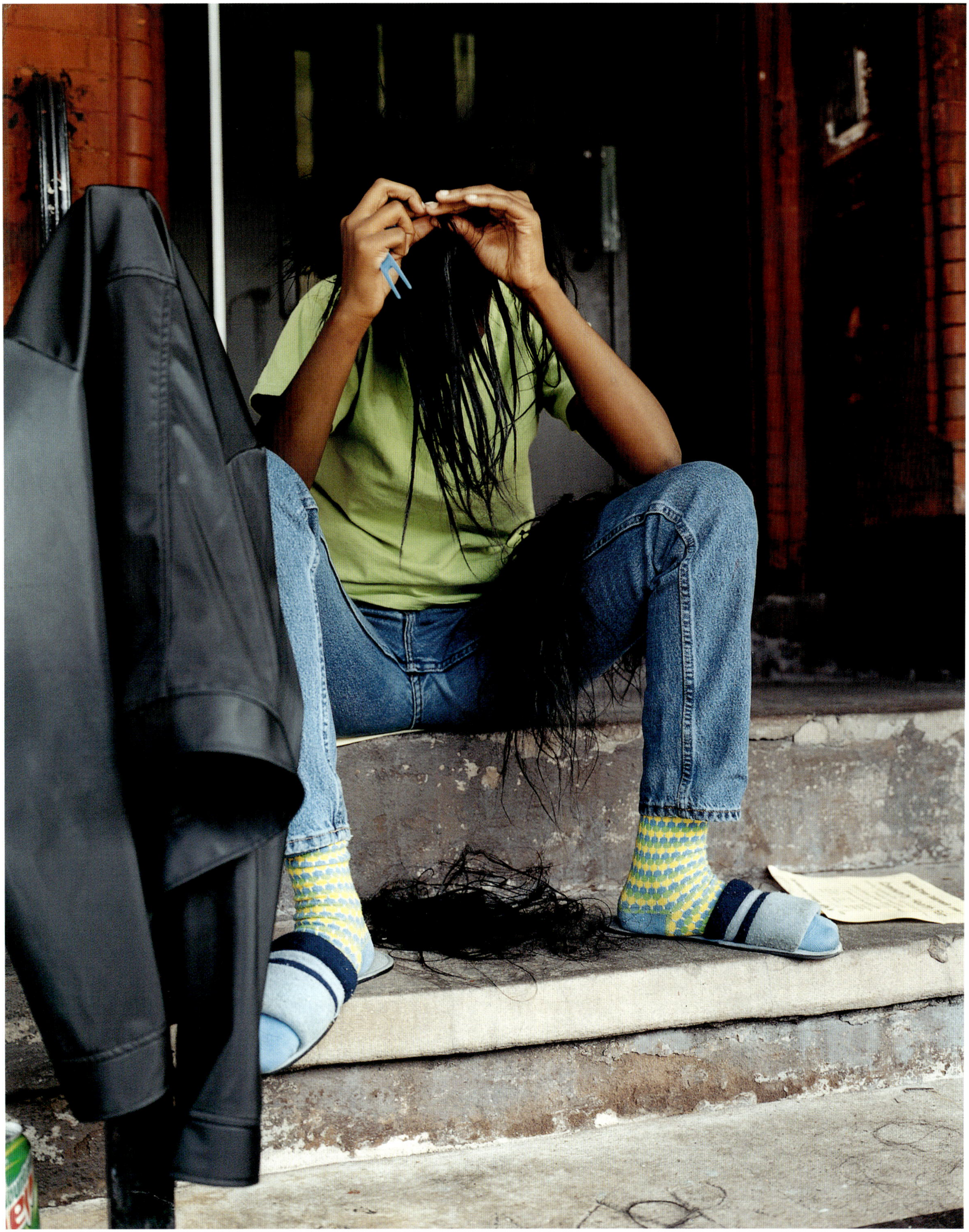

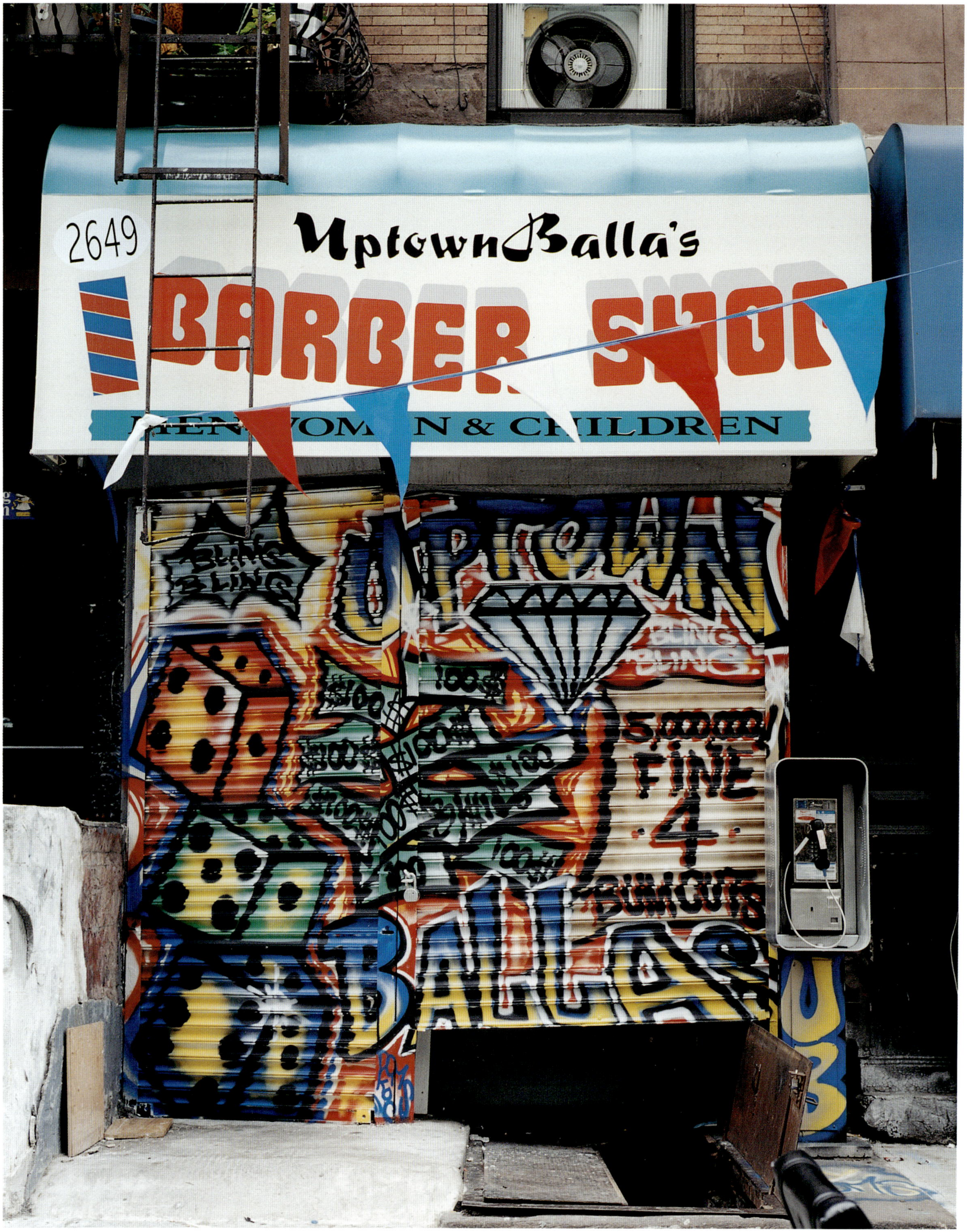
2649
UptownBalla's
BARBER SHOP
N & CHILDREN
BLING BLING
BLING BLING
FINE
4
BUM CUTS

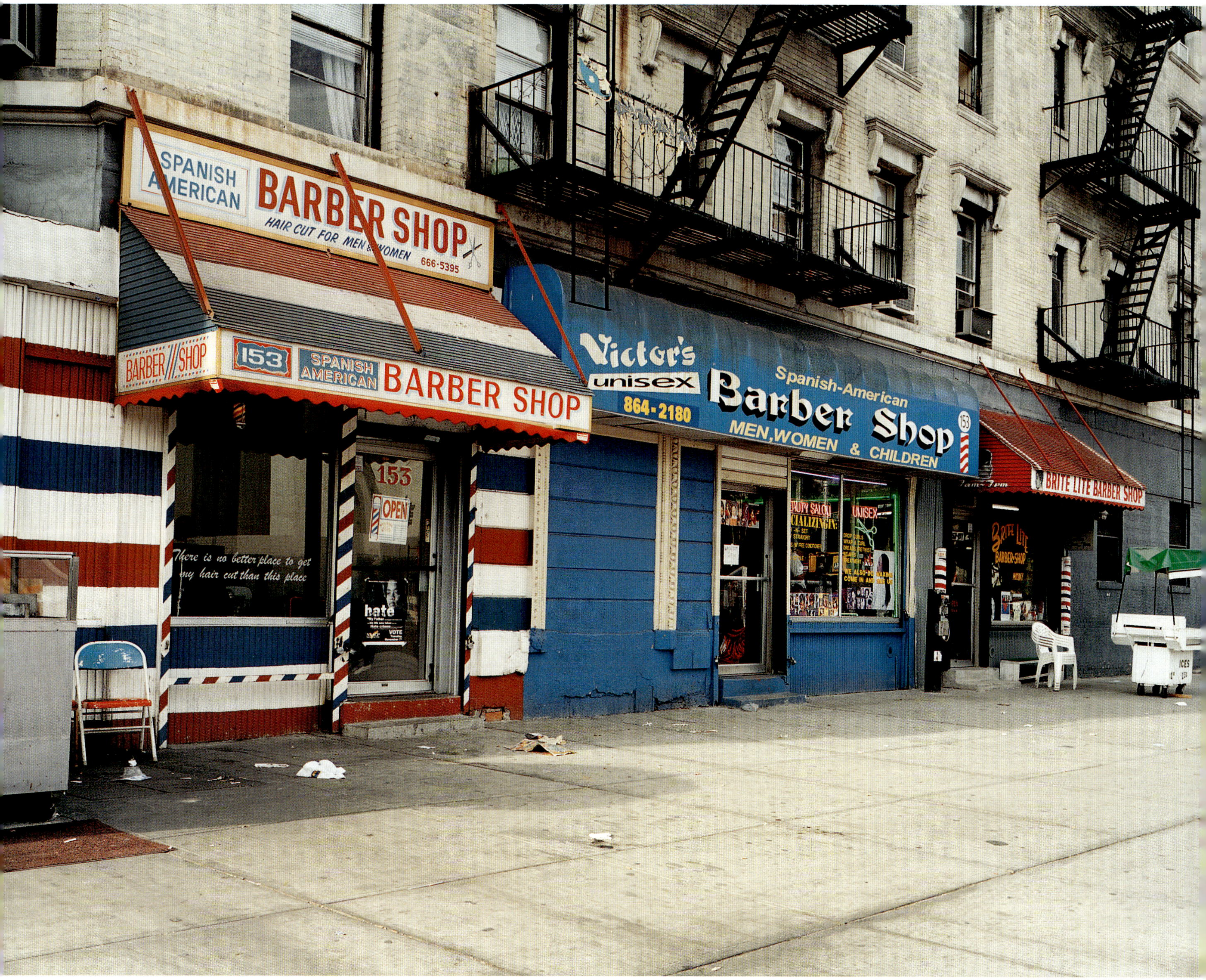
SPANISH AMERICAN BARBER SHOP
HAIR CUT FOR MEN & WOMEN
666-5395
BARBER SHOP
153
SPANISH AMERICAN BARBER SHOP
153
OPEN
There is no better place to get my hair cut than this place
hate
VOTE
Victor's
unisex
864-2180
Spanish-American
Barber Shop
MEN, WOMEN & CHILDREN
153
UNISEX
BRITE LITE BARBER SHOP
ICES

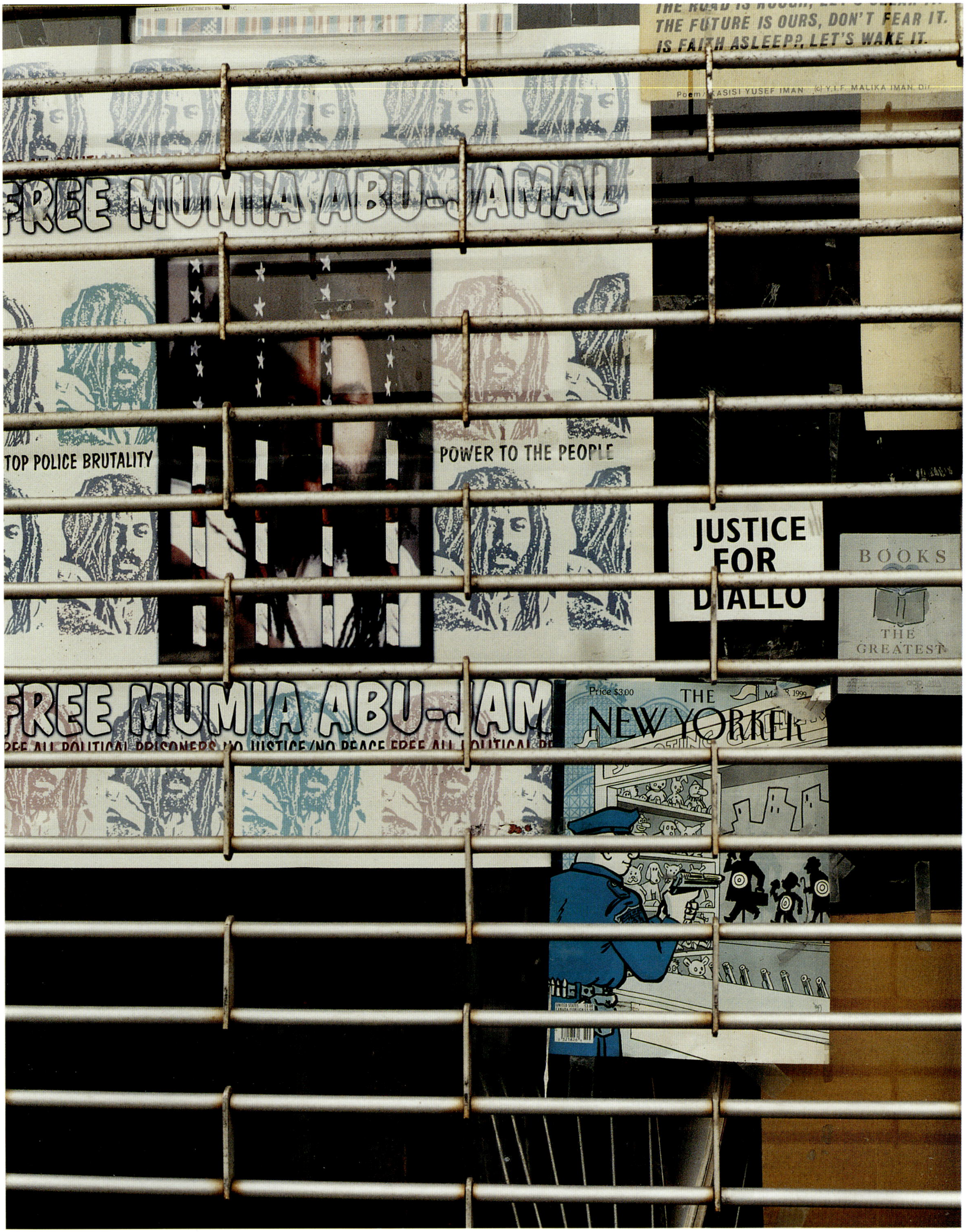
THE FUTURE IS OURS, DON'T FEAR IT.
IS FAITH ASLEEP?, LET'S WAKE IT.
FREE MUMIA ABU-JAMAL
TOP POLICE BRUTALITY
POWER TO THE PEOPLE
JUSTICE FOR DIALLO
BOOKS
THE GREATEST
FREE MUMIA ABU-JAM
Price $3.00
THE NEW YORKER

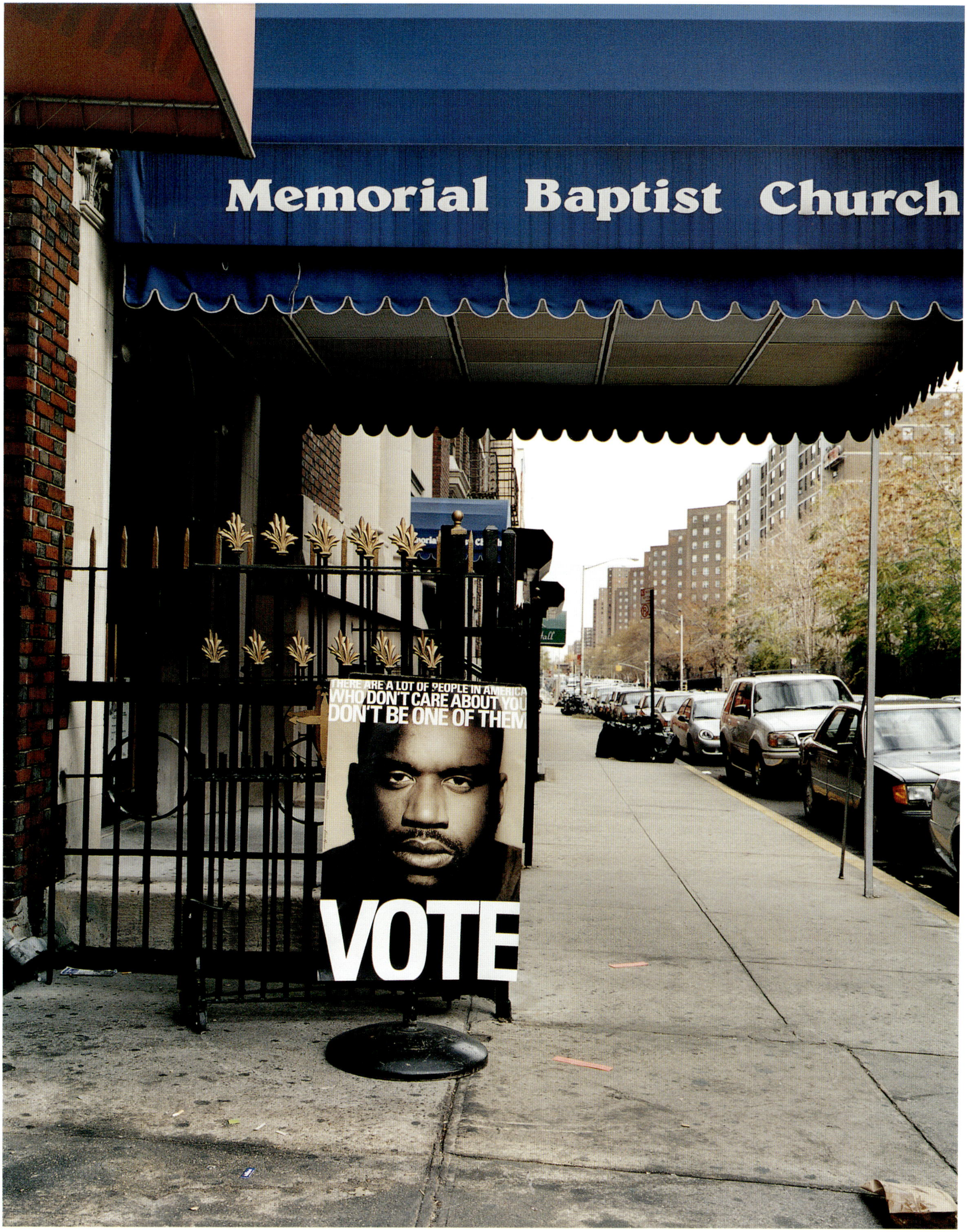
Memorial Baptist Church
THERE ARE A LOT OF PEOPLE IN AMERICA
WHO DON'T CARE ABOUT YOU
DON'T BE ONE OF THEM
VOTE

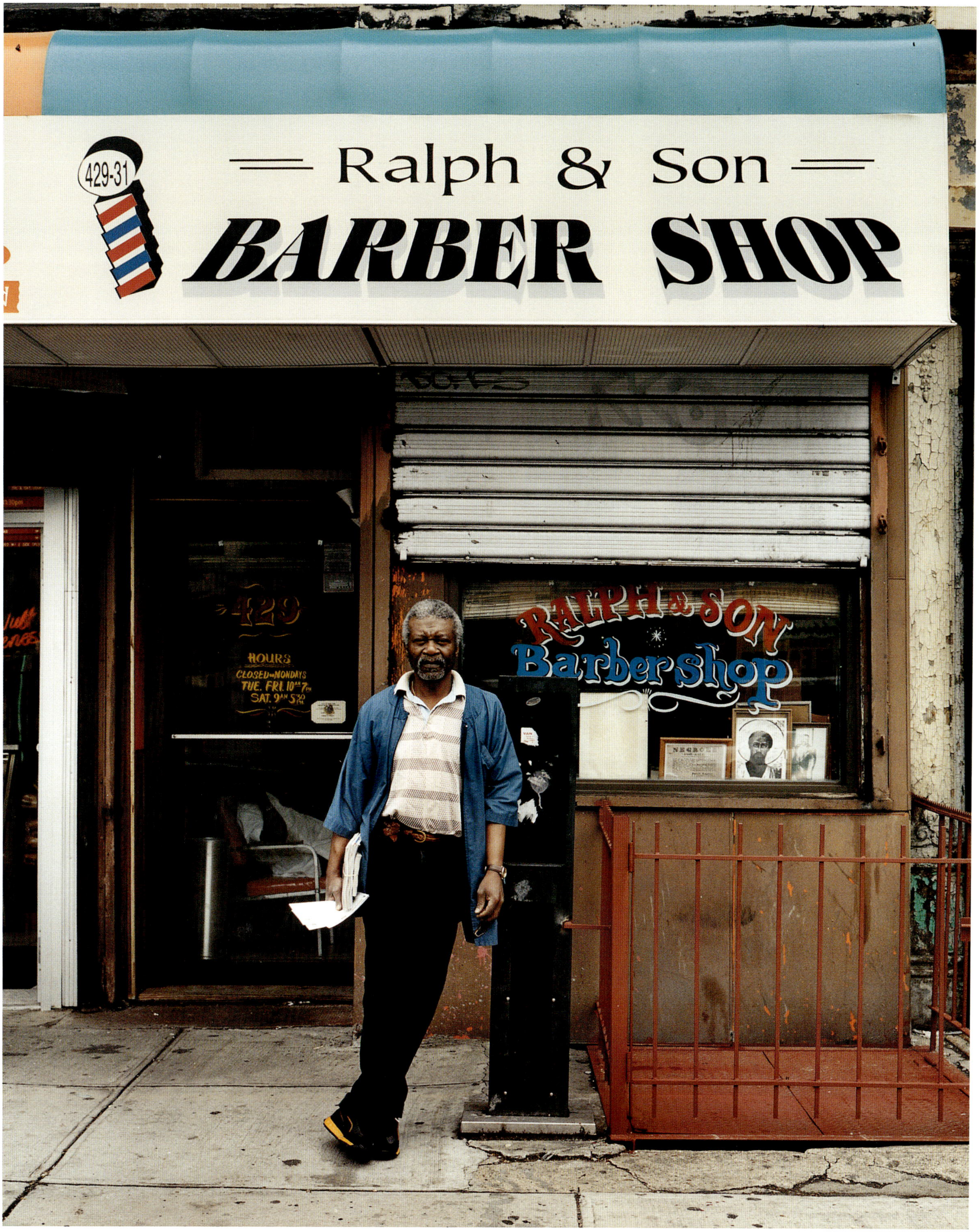
429-31
Ralph & Son
BARBER SHOP
RALPH & SON
Barbershop
HOURS
CLOSED MONDAYS
TUE. FRI. 10AM 7PM
SAT. 9AM 5:30PM

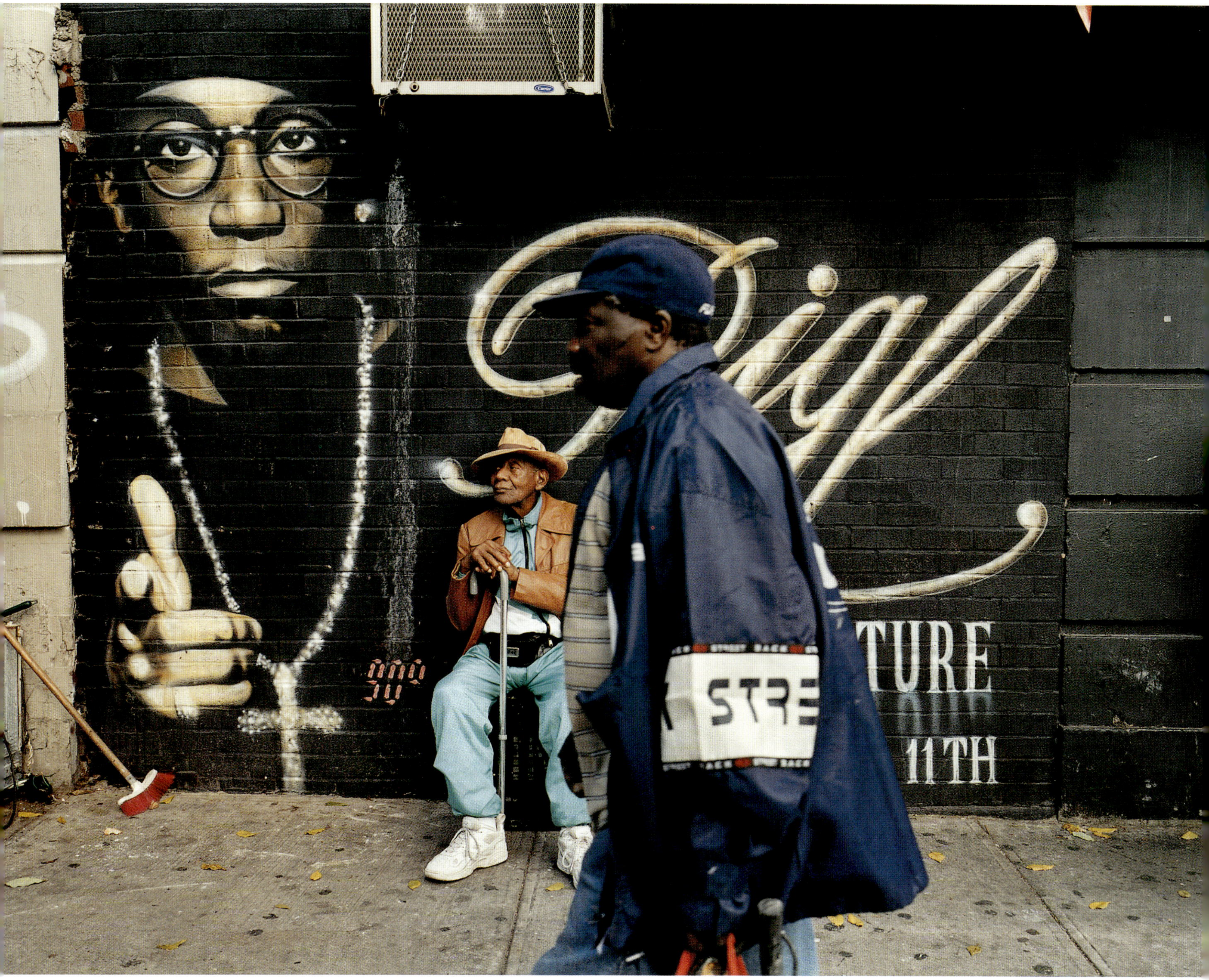
TURE
11TH

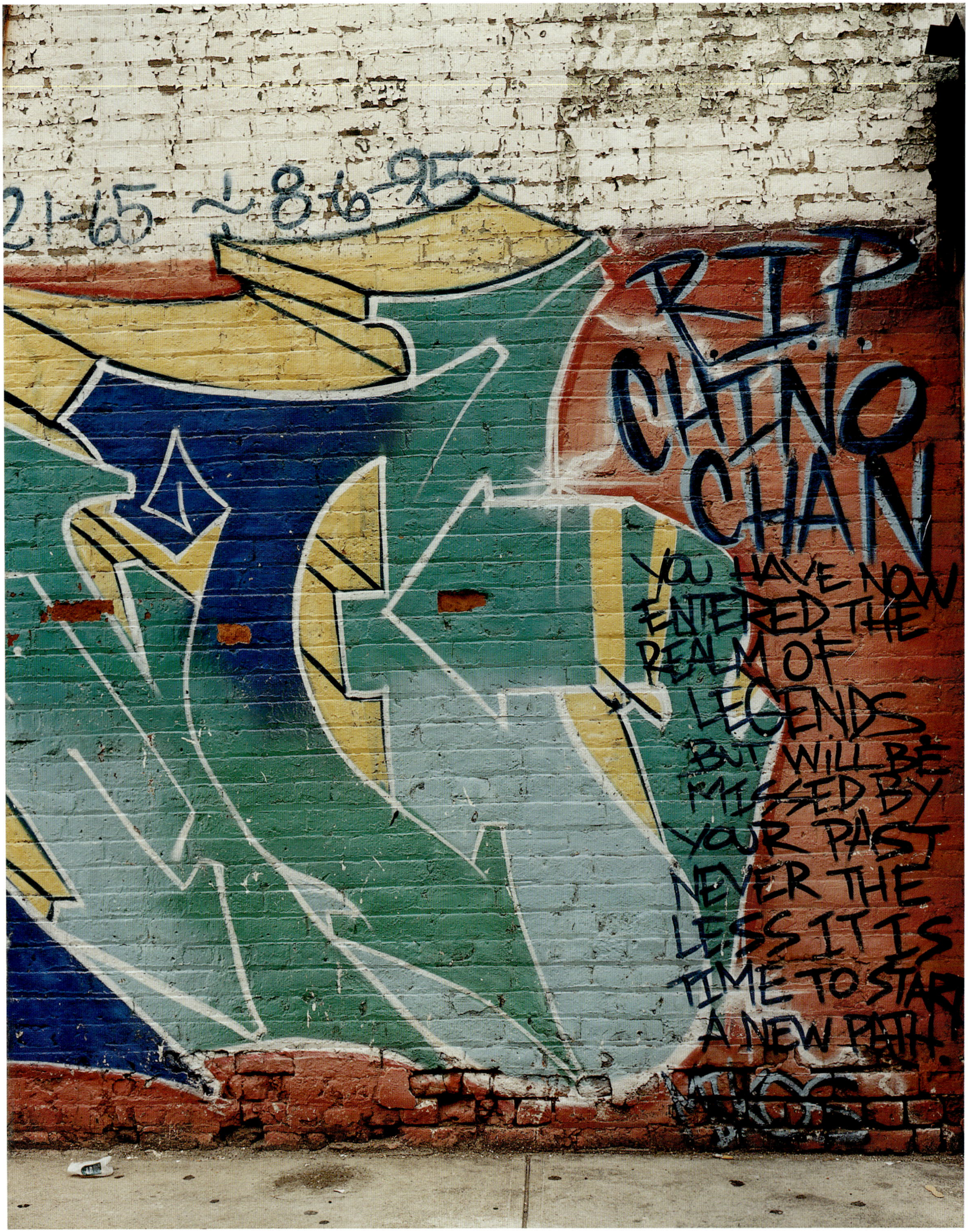
21-65 ~ 8-6-95
R.I.P.
CHINO
CHAN
YOU HAVE NOW ENTERED THE REALM OF LEGENDS BUT WILL BE MISSED BY YOUR PAST NEVER THE LESS IT IS TIME TO START A NEW PATH.

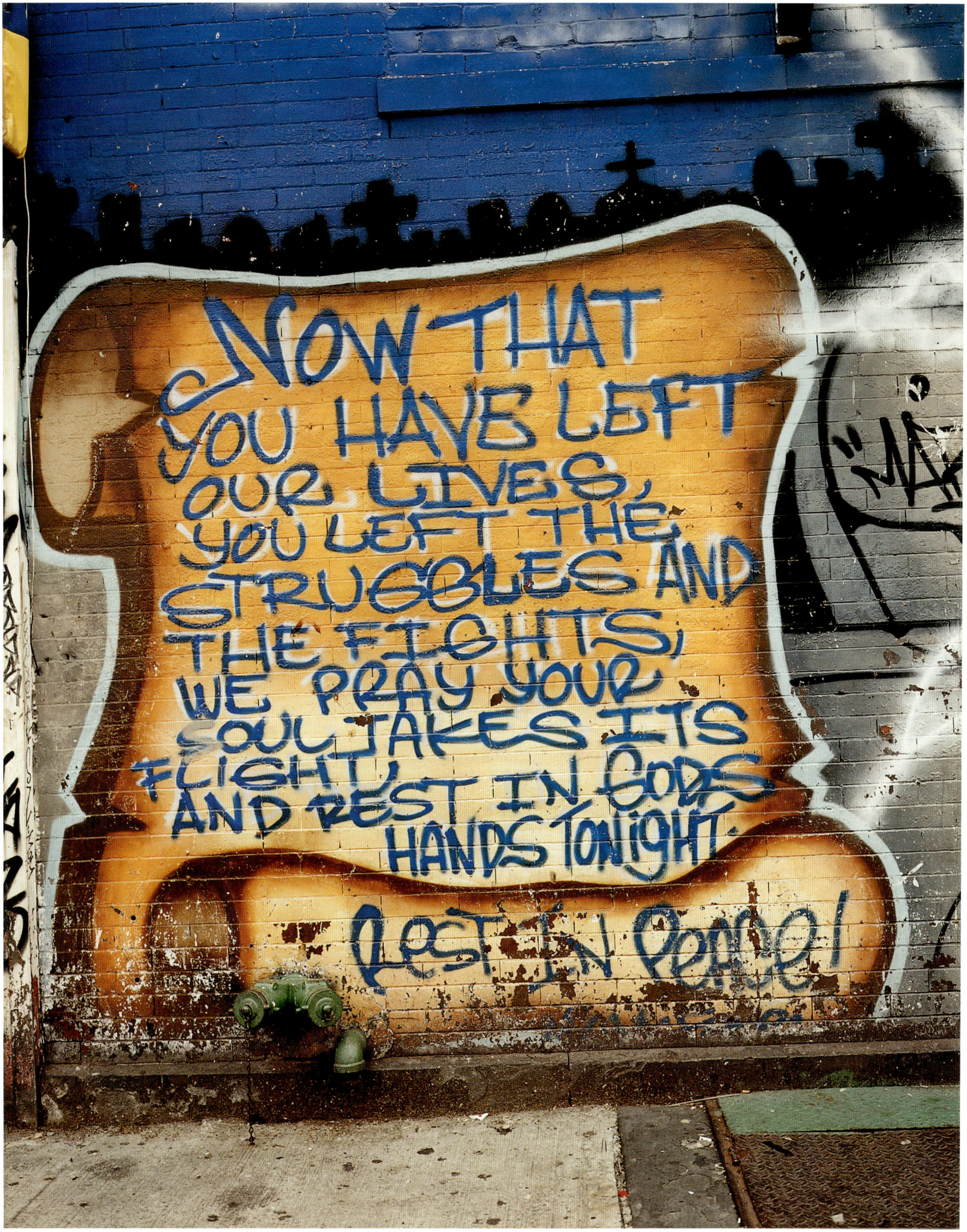
NOW THAT
YOU HAVE LEFT
OUR LIVES,
YOU LEFT THE
STRUGGLES AND
THE FIGHTS,
WE PRAY YOUR
SOUL TAKES ITS
FLIGHT
AND REST IN GODS
HANDS TONIGHT.
Rest In Peace!

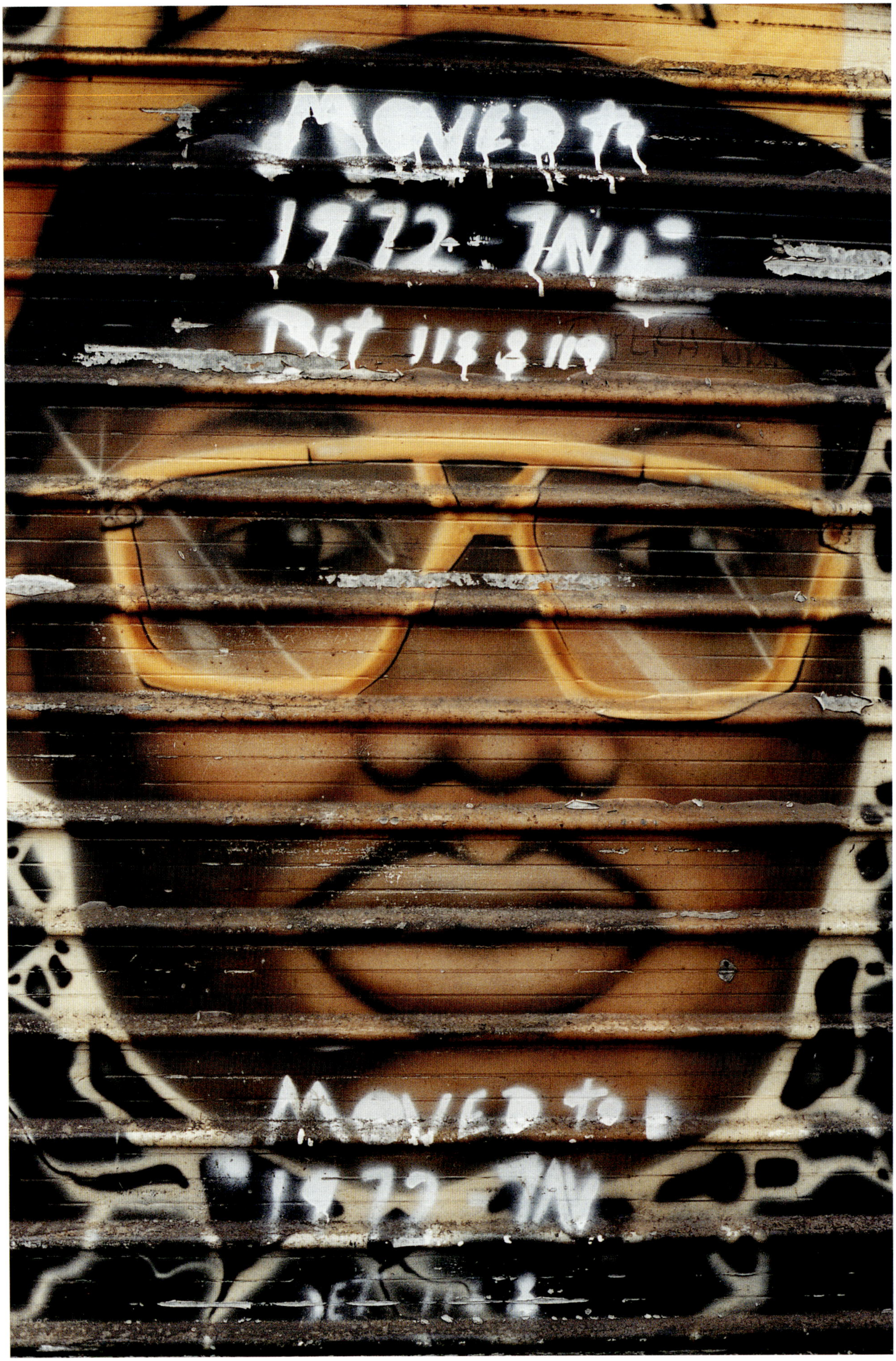
MOVED to
1772 7AV
Bet 118 & 119

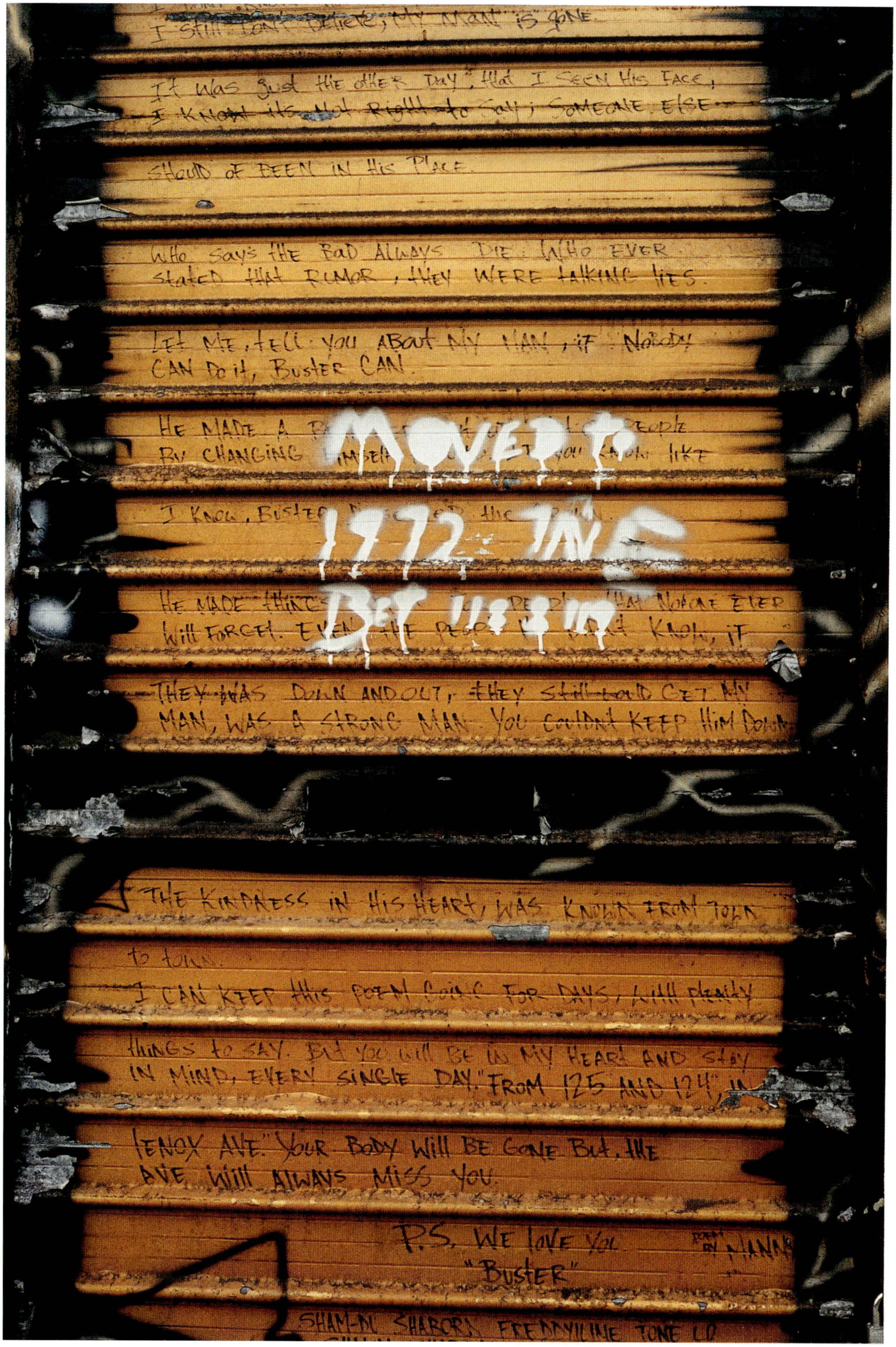
I still can't believe, my man is gone
It was just the other day, that I seen his face,
I know it's not right to say, someone else
should of been in his place.
Who says the bad always die, who ever
stated that rumor, they were talking lies.
Let me tell you about my man, if nobody
can do it, Buster can.
MAN, WAS A STRONG MAN. YOU COULDN'T KEEP HIM DOWN
The kindness in his heart, was known from town
to town.
I can keep this poem going for days, with plenty
things to say. But you will be in my heart and stay
in mind, every single day. From 125 and 124, in
Lenox Ave. Your body will be gone but, the
Ave will always miss you.
P.S. We love you
"Buster"

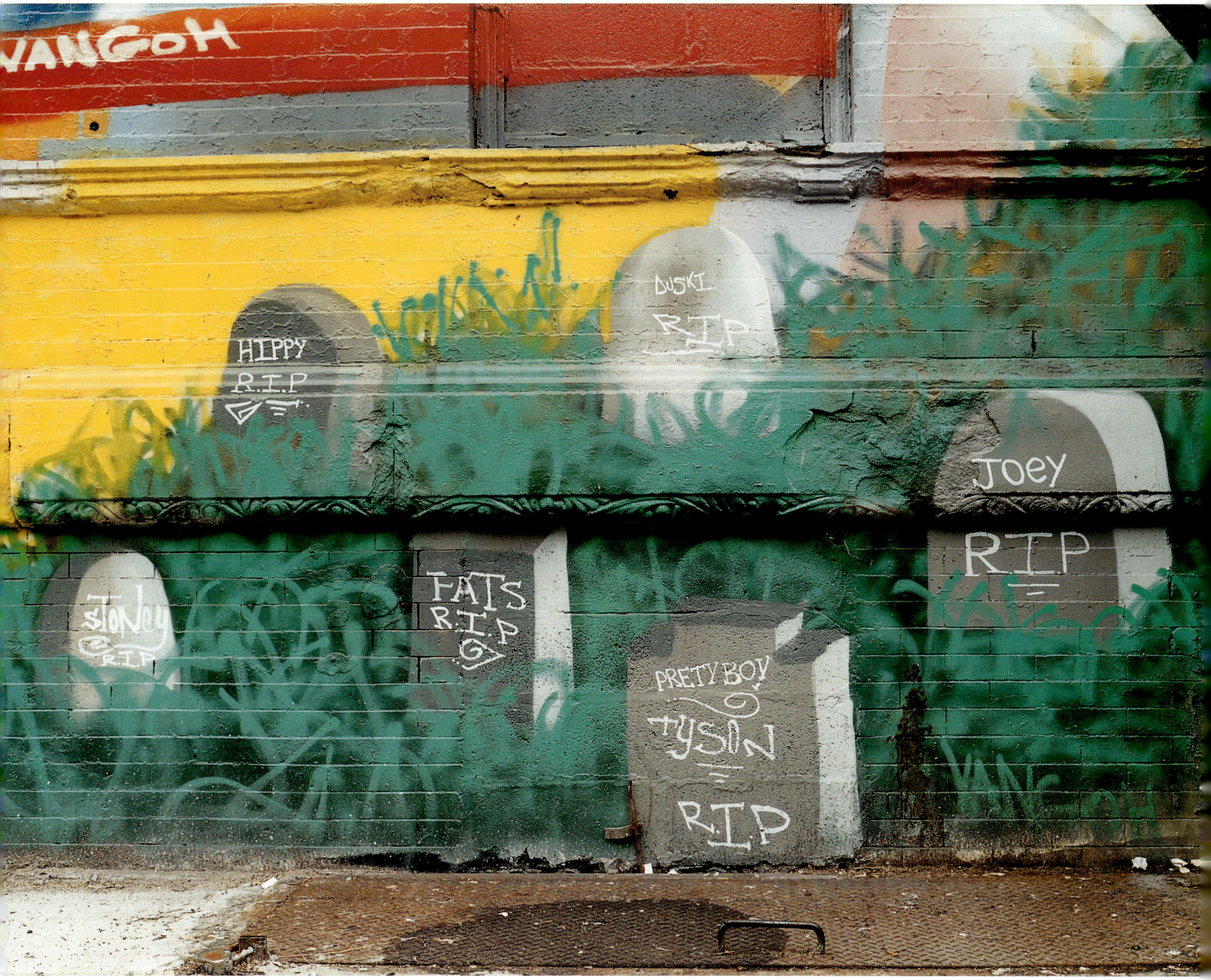
VANGOH
HIPPY
R.I.P
DUSKI
R.I.P
Joey
RIP
stoney
R.I.P
FATS
R.I.P
PRETY BOY
TYSON
R.I.P

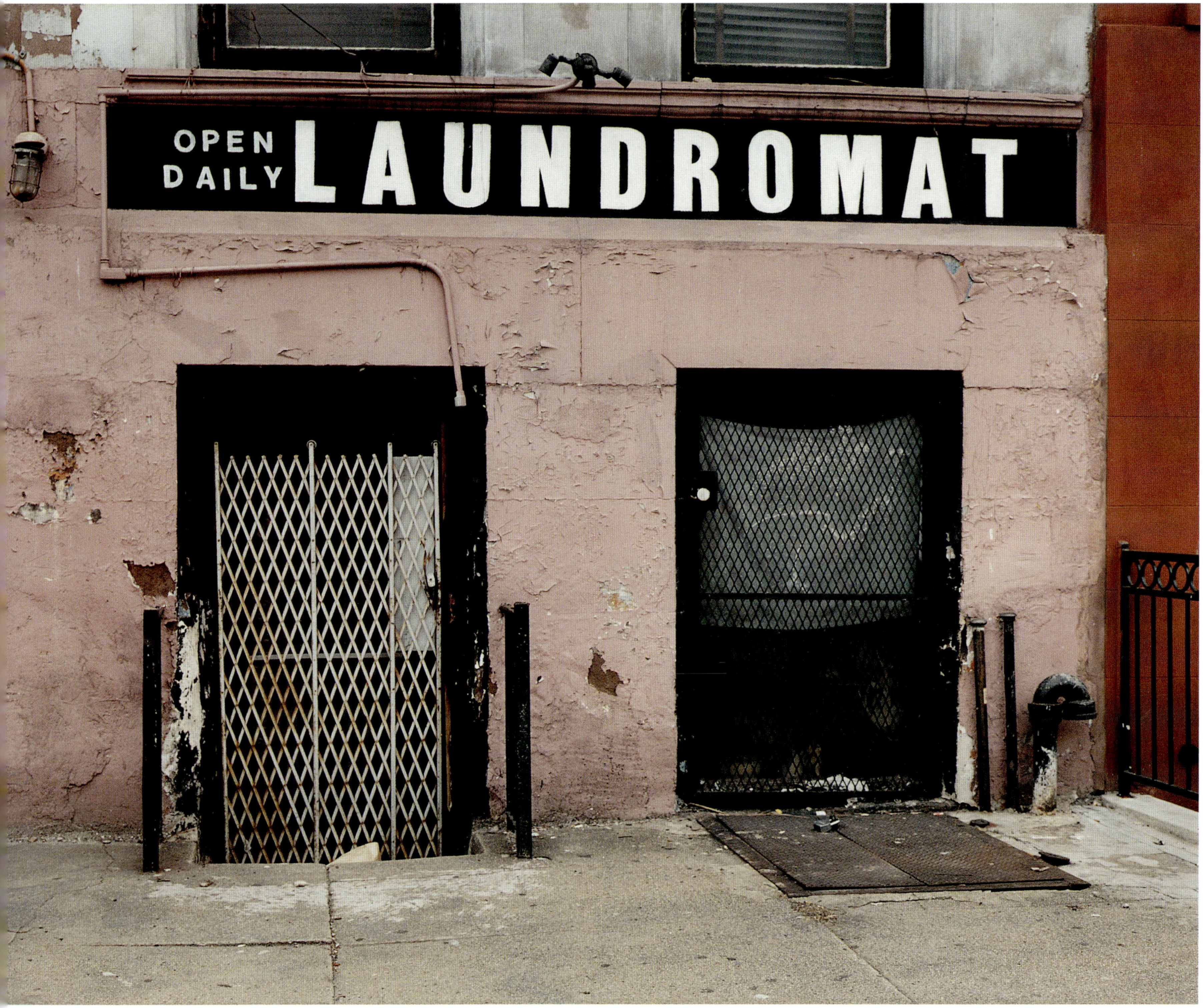
OPEN
DAILY
LAUNDROMAT

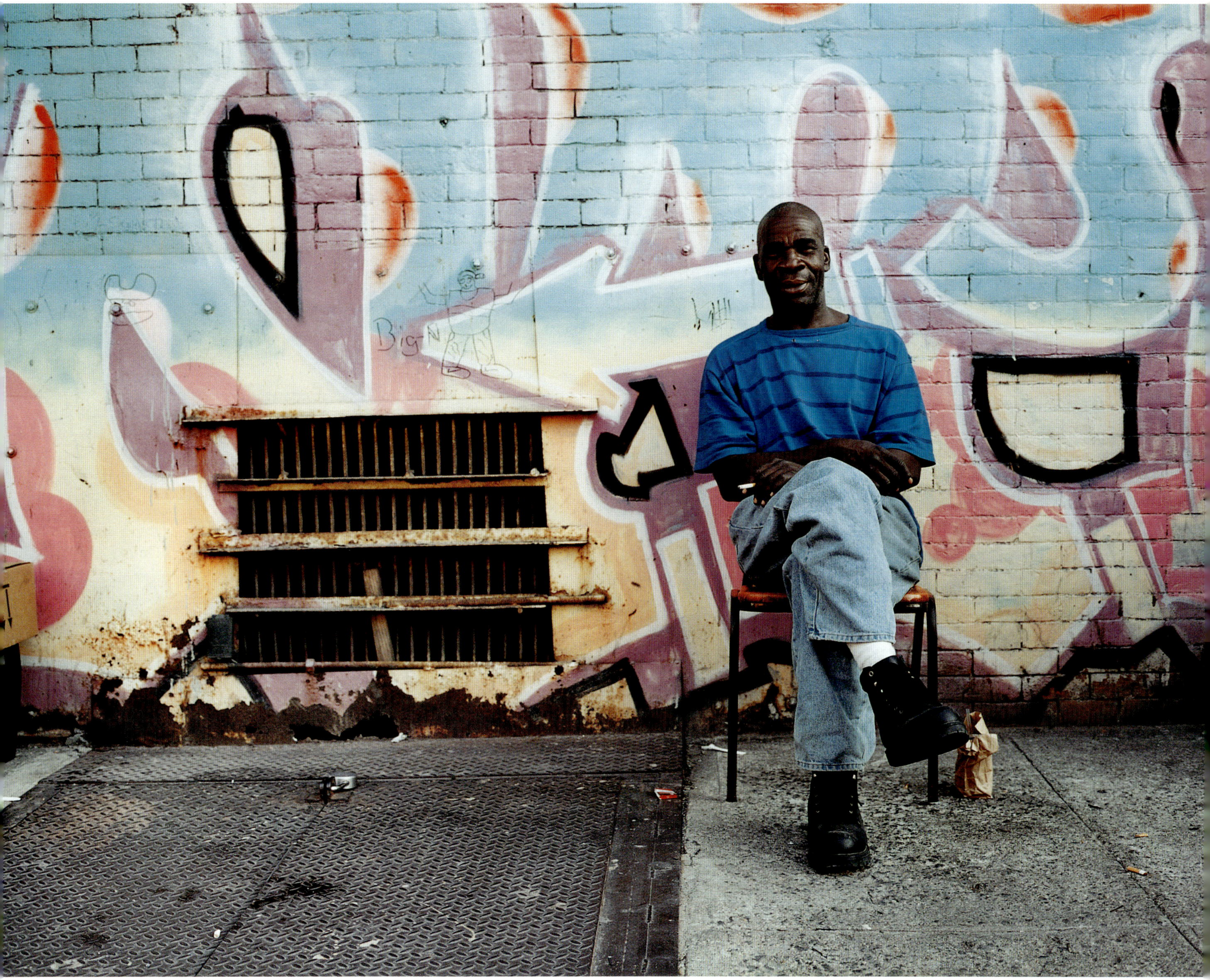

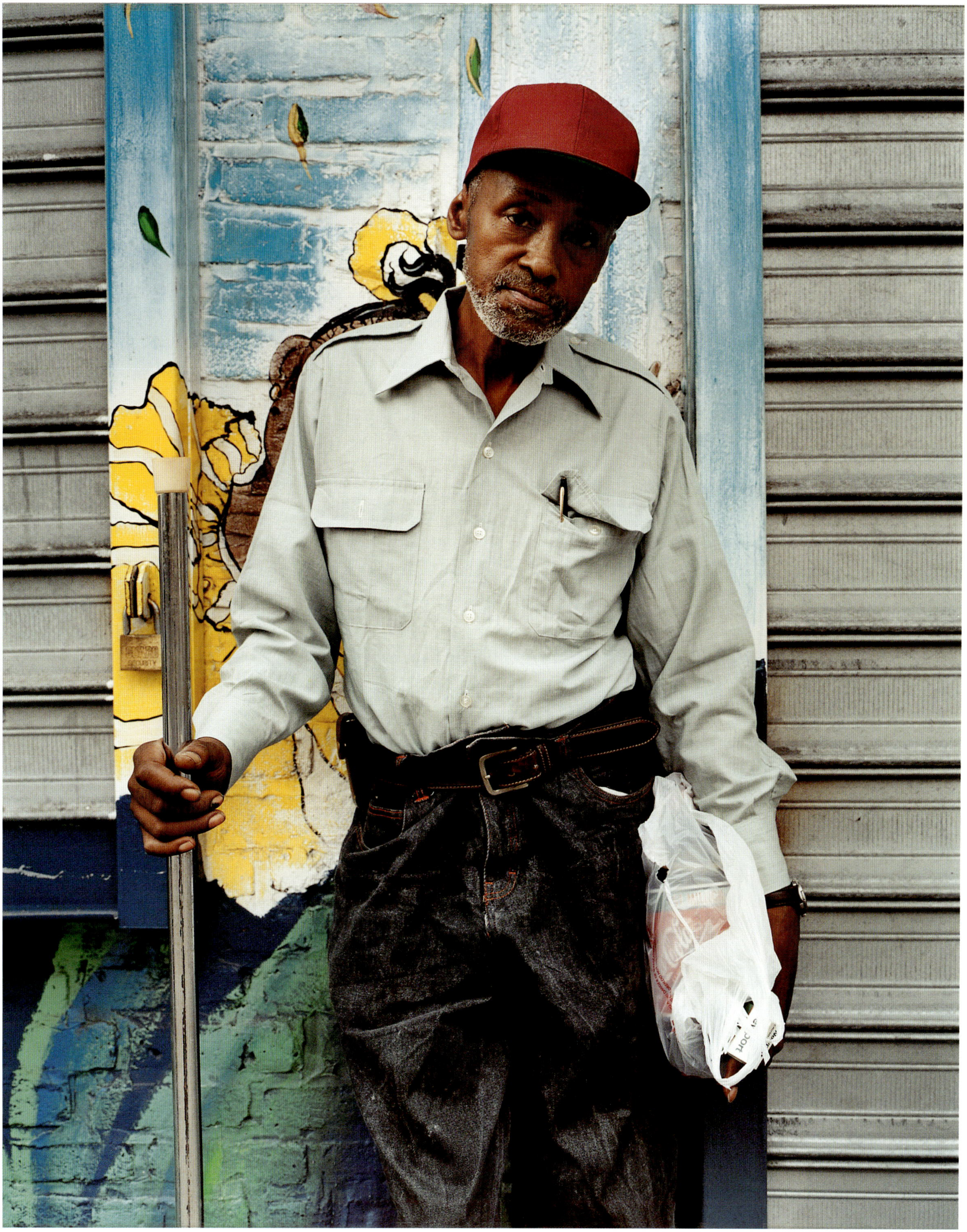

A changing Harlem holds still for the memory.
With joy and with sadness the people look at you.
Are they thinking about what was or how it is going to be?

An iron shutter locks the building—it says *MOVED*

"Your baby will be gone but the avenue will always miss you"

With sympathy and open eye, Alice Attie tells us about life in America.

ROBERT FRANK

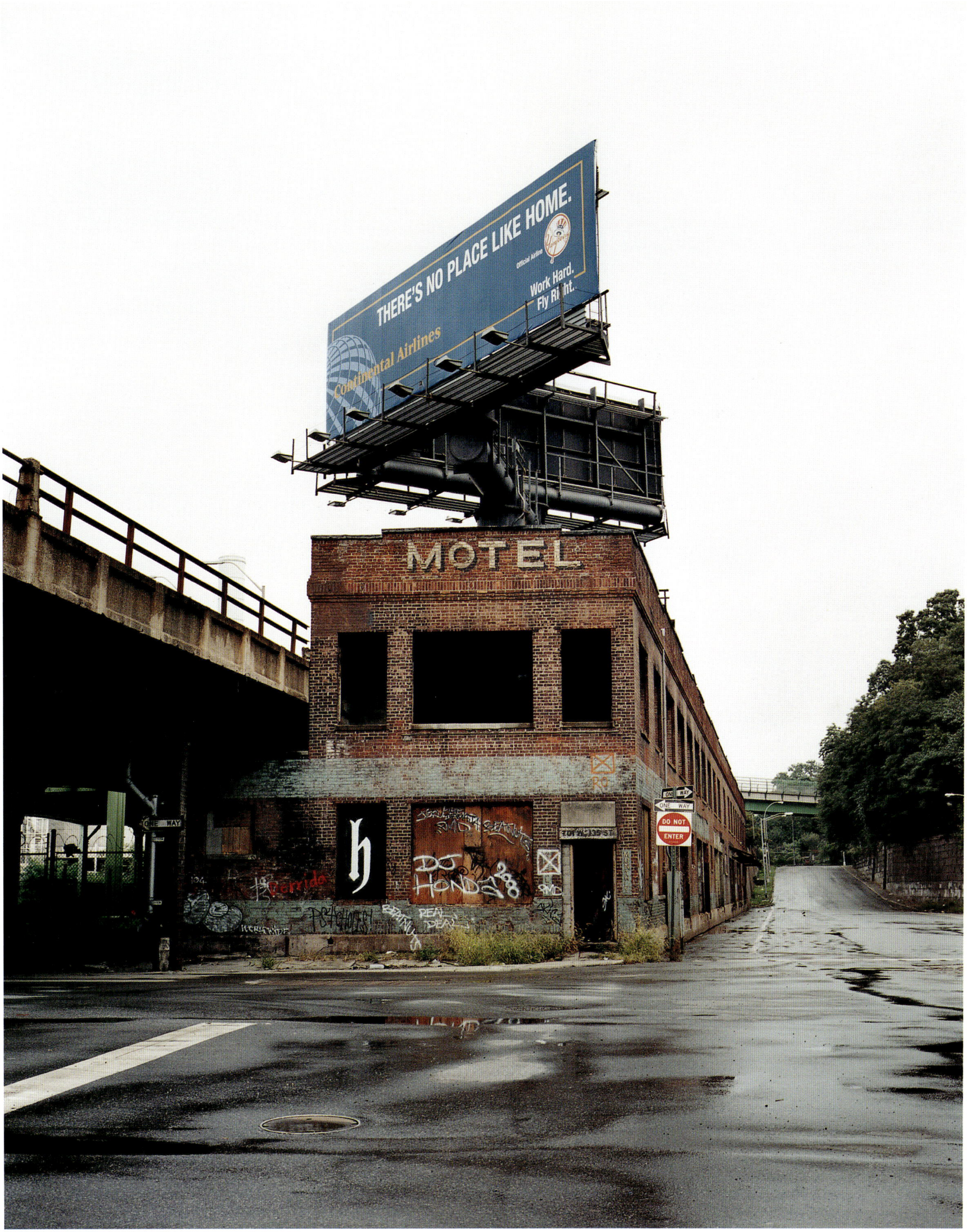
THERE'S NO PLACE LIKE HOME.
Continental Airlines
Official Airline
Work Hard.
Fly Right.
MOTEL
ONE WAY
DO NOT
ENTER

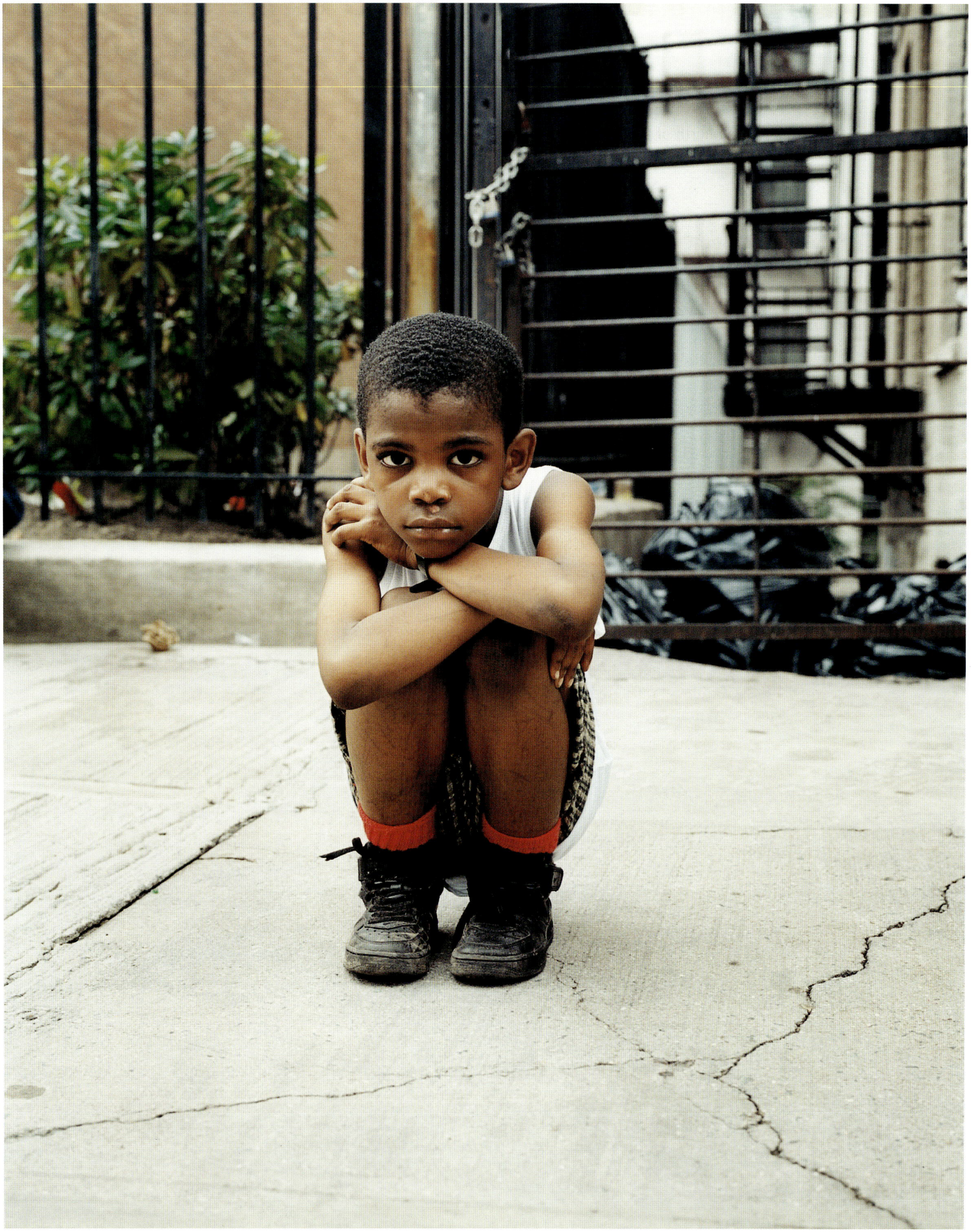

AFTERWORD

Harlem is situated north of Central Park, in New York City—its broad boulevards and dramatic hills span over fifty city blocks. Historically, this African American community has been defined both by its rich history and by its struggle to thrive within the confines of a city whose economic delineations have kept it, while part of the city, in many ways secluded from it. In the spring of 2000, crossing 125th Street on the bus to La Guardia Airport, I noticed that Disney had opened a store in Harlem. As the bus wove from west to east, what I saw felt more and more ominous. For the following year I ventured up to Harlem, a community I have lived in close proximity to for many years, almost daily, by bicycle. Initially, I set out to document the closing of small neighborhood shops and the appearance of large corporate retailers; gradually the project grew to be a study of the community itself, the faces of its residents, its shops, its avenues and its historic landmarks. As I wandered the streets, residents spoke with me about their concerns for the future; they shared their stories and their memories of a community that they felt was being threatened. They continually helped me, as an outsider and "other," to understand what is at stake in the sudden burst of economic interest in the community.

As Harlem confronts the pressures of "development," it is being forced to redefine itself, and issues of isolation and integration have taken on new meanings. This redefinition has a profoundly visual component. From the signage on the storefronts to the memorials on the walls, Harlem residents have inscribed the complex range of their cultural identities onto the streets of their neighborhoods. The economic forces which are altering the landscape of urban and suburban America, have a particular resonance for the capital of African America.

The challenge, to individuals and communities alike, is to understand what the larger forces of global capital mean to the small entrepreneur and to the social fabric of communities. As we become accustomed to proliferation of corporate logos, to the dissemination of chain stores throughout the country and the world, we grow used to an onslaught of images which fall upon us, generating new needs and offering seductive means for satisfying them. In a community where ownership of property has always rested with outsiders, these new enterprises represent troubling new forces. Corporations are faceless; they have no identifiable ethnicity; yet they appear to young hip consumers to be familiar neighbors. Yet, the homogenization of consumption works in subtle ways. In a community such as Harlem, where a sense of place and a sense of having access to public space is essential to the concept of community itself, the process becomes one of *erasure*. The creatively adorned shops, *Tony's Laundry, 43rd Street Records, Livingston Productions, Angies, Uptown Balla, Mikes Stand and Land, The Princess Lounge*, are the Davids that face the Goliaths of displacement. As the family-owned shop struggles to survive throughout the city, as the bodega, the tailor, the cleaner, the coffee shop, the bookstore disappear, we begin to register what is being sacrificed. In March of 2003, two years after my project began, traveling up to Harlem to look at the sites I had photographed I found more than half of them were gone. These are losses that signify not merely the transitory nature of the urban landscape but threats to the very concept of ethnic diversity.

This transformative moment in Harlem has larger implications for a world in which small communities increasingly confront the tyranny of corporate interests. I often think about Walter Benjamin's premonition that there may come a day when the idea of *duration* will cease to matter, when the photograph may not only document the passage of time but will stand for the disappearance of an *aura,* a sense of the irreplaceable. Wrestling with the many ways of reading a photograph, Benjamin suggested that it is by way of the image that the culture's memory passes through the eye. The photograph becomes the mark of a crisis, a rupture and the beginning of historical mourning. The fragility of the urban landscape, like the fragility of the writings on the walls, is suspended by another equally fragile medium—photography. Photographing the people and the streets of Harlem has been my effort to honor the rich culture embedded in the landscape of this remarkable community. The tremendous vitality and spirit of Harlem's residents, their strength and their courage, continue to inspire me.

ACKNOWLEDGEMENTS

My heartfelt thanks to the residents of Harlem for inviting me into their shops, their homes, their lives. There is little I could say that could convey the warmth and comraderie that welcomed me throughout my year in Harlem. It has been one of the most extraordinary experiences of my life.

I would like to thank Jim Mairs, my editor at Quantuck Lane Press, who believed in this project from the beginning. Jim's friendship and humor have helped to make this book more than I could have ever hoped for. Thanks to Katy Homans for her keen eye in assisting the design of this book, and to Brook Wilensky-Lanford for her tireless editorial work. Many thanks to Richard Woodward for launching this work in *Doubletake* Magazine. Rick's encouragement and his insights helped form the bedrock of my Harlem project. My heartfelt thanks to Robin Kelley; Robin's fervor, his indefatigable effort to say what needs to to be said, stands alone and is exemplary. My gratitude to my dear friend, the late Phima Englestein; her wisdom has fortified me for years. Thanks to Aaron Kahn, a rare friend and a generous critic. My appreciation to Robert Peacock whose energy and perseverance guided me in the initial stages of envisioning this book. My gratitude to Gayatri Spivak is immense; she took this project to Germany, to England, to Brazil, and back home to Columbia University. Gayatri's intellectual fortitude continues to stagger me. Her understanding of these images as visual meditations on questions of endurance and displacement have helped me to see their global significance. To Jonathan Lewis, whose love, vision, humor, and, not in the least, karma, have lit my way so many times. For June Jordan, African American poet and activist. Not long ago, June began a series of poems about her childhood in Harlem which she hoped to contribute to this book. Although cancer cut June's life short, the power of her voice is with me, in these images, as it is in the lives of everyone who knew her. I owe tremendous thanks to Robert Frank for spending generous time with this work. Robert represents, for me, what it means to have integrity behind the lens of a camera.

My gratitude to the following individuals who help me through so many aspects of this work. I would like to thank Gordon Spencer, dive coach, lifeguard, dear friend and critic, for his invaluable input; Dennis Kuronen, Jean Foos, and Eileen Boxer for their assistance envisioning the cover of this book; Martin Peterson and Chriswell Lapin at *Metropolis* Magazine; Betsy Urrico-Brandes at *Doubletake* magazine; Sylvia Curbela at *Organica* Magazine; Reinhold Martin at *Grey Room*; Sami Georgy at Columbia Copy Center. To the entire staff of the Neiman Art Gallery at Columbia University, many thanks for exhibiting this work. My deep appreciation to Brian Wallis for his generous time and encouragement.

Without the immeasurable love of my family, who has understood my varied photographic journeys for so many years, this book would never have happened. Enormous thanks to my sister Ilana, my brother Kenny, my cousin Shimon, my aunt Dotty, and my uncle Stephen. A great appreciation to my sister Jeanie, whose political activisim and brilliant editing skills kept and keep me alert at all times.

My children, Justine and Gideon Kahn, will always guide me. I turn to them constantly. They are tough; they are tender, endlessly tolerant, and profoundly wise. At each stage of this project, I shared experiences and photographs with them; their input and inquiries were invaluable.

Gratitude to Royce Howes, my love, my partner in life, my confidant. He has supported me in all of my projects, at all times. I thank him for working tirelessly to fine tune the difficult decisions around this book, and for understanding my need to journey to other side, to see further than the eye's first glimpse. I could not have pulled this book together without Royce's love.

I dedicate this book, first and foremost, to my parents. From an early age, they taught me the ongoing challenge that comprises one's life work, that one's individual struggle is ultimately a universal one. They helped me to understand that art can and does change the world. They encouraged me to venture out beyond the familiar, to trust and to find beauty in things difficult, to embrace what I least understand.

To my father, Joseph Attie, photographer, surgeon and humanist, I dedicate this book. His extraordinary belief in the magnificence of life will never cease to inspire me. He did not live to see this body of work come to print but in every image there hides an homage to his vision, his compassion and his sense of wonder.

To Muriel Attie, for whom there are few words adequate to express the respect, the love and the awe I feel, I dedicate this book. She has been my role model; she has given me the insights, the critical eye, and the political fervor that propel me through my life. Were it not for my mother, I may never have understood the nature of true commitment, that it never wavers, that it is continually enriched by one's compassion, one's vision, and one's imagination.

ALICE ATTIE

The photographs in this book were taken with a Mamiya 7 II camera using Kodak Portra 400 NC film.
They were printed at Hong Color in New York City;
my special thanks to Ben and Lou Diep for their extraordinary work.

I could not have covered the length and breadth of Harlem without my bicycle.
My gratitude to Trek Bicycles.